Tracey Whitmore is an entrepreneur, author and CV-writing professional with a background in recruitment, online retail and financial services.

Passionate about helping people and making a difference, she launched and ran Impressive CVs, a professional CV-writing business in 2003. Together with her team, she created interview-winning CVs helping more than two thousand clients secure their dream job. Over a seven-year period, she amassed hundreds of testimonials on the impact her CVs made to people's job hunt and career. She subsequently sold the business.

In response to the coronavirus pandemic, she has relaunched herself as 'The CV Doctor' (www.theCVdoctor.co.uk) to help get people back to work. She is again focused on writing compelling, tailored-made CVs for people from all levels, industries and backgrounds.

In her early career, she worked as a headhunter for a boutique firm of search consultants where she placed several senior managers in the financial services and insurance sectors. Prior to this, she worked as a credit analyst for Deutsche Bank, Coutts & Co and BNP Paribas.

Originally from South Africa, she is educated to degree level with a Bachelor of Commerce from UNISA. She now lives in Luton with her husband, two beautiful kids, Cade and Erin, and their dog Roxy.

She recently joined Toastmasters, not to make toast, but to learn the art of public speaking. She has become an avid runner, enjoys tennis, cross-stitch and walking the dog.

TRACEY WHITMORE

HOW TO WRITE AN IMPRESSIVE CV & COVER LETTER

A COMPREHENSIVE GUIDE FOR JOBSEEKERS

A How To book

ROBINSON

ROBINSON

First published in Great Britain in 2009 by
How To Books

This revised edition published in 2021 by
Robinson

10 9 8 7 6 5 4 3 2 1

A CIP catalogue record for this book
is available from the British Library.

ISBN: 978-1-4721-4535-2

Typeset in Sentinel and Scala Sans
by Ian Hughes

Printed and bound in Great Britain by Clays
Ltd, Elcograf S.p.A.

Papers used by Robinson are from well-
managed forests and other responsible
sources.

FSC
www.fsc.org

MIX
Paper from
responsible sources
FSC® C104740

Robinson
An imprint of
Little, Brown Book Group
Carmelite House
50 Victoria Embankment
London EC4Y 0DZ

An Hachette UK Company
www.hachette.co.uk

www.littlebrown.co.uk

How To Books are published by
Robinson, an imprint of Little, Brown
Book Group. We welcome proposals
from authors who have first-hand
experience of their subjects. Please set
out the aims of your book, its target
market and its suggested contents in an
email to howto@littlebrown.co.uk.

Contents

Introduction

This book is four rolled into one and aims to support the UK jobseeker through the entire job-hunting process. It will take the reader on a journey from mentally preparing for finding/changing job, through to how to write an impressive CV, cover letter and LinkedIn profile. Useful tips from industry leaders are provided throughout as well as real-life examples of CVs and cover letters that have won interviews. These, together with valuable templates, are hosted online.

The book is divided into four distinct parts, each of which will be discussed in more detail.

Part One: The Job-hunting Process

This section covers the job-hunting process. It begins with mental preparation and ends with embracing change. It examines how to decide on your target role, the importance of bridging skills or qualification gaps and then touches upon writing your CV, cover letter and LinkedIn profile, which are covered in detail in Parts Two, Three and Four.

Part Two: CV Writing

The first two chapters examine what a CV is, the importance of getting it right and the different CV types. The chapters that follow are each dedicated to a specific CV component from heading your CV through to the 'Additional Information' section. Where appropriate, the chapter will distinguish between information required for an entry-level job seeker versus someone with more experience. Format, structure and presentation are then considered. The penultimate chapter covers real-life CVs struggling to win interviews, followed by the actual CV that resulted in the job offer.

Part Three: LinkedIn Profile Writing

Given the significance of LinkedIn in the job-hunting process, this section is a new addition. It encompasses a step-by-step process to writing your own profile, including the importance of keywords and endorsements.

Part Four: Cover Letter Writing

This section covers the importance of a cover letter, the marks of a good one and the difference between a speculative and specific cover letter. The penultimate chapter assesses real-life cover letters that have been successful.

What Sets this Book Apart?

As should be the case with a CV, this book has several USPs (unique selling points).

First, it comprises CVs and cover letters that have been successful in real life. These are available to view both in the book and others are hosted online. With customer permissions, this will be added to for the foreseeable future.

Second, it provides a selection of CV and cover letter templates which are hosted online and will be updated as times change.

Third, the book includes the viewpoints of senior HR professionals from the likes of Accenture, BBC, Vodafone and Spencer Stewart allowing us to glean an insight into the whole job acquisition process. Additionally, fellow CV-writing professionals have been consulted. Their comments and input are embraced to provide the reader with a rounded viewpoint.

Fourth, practical examples are offered at each stage of the process to provide the reader with inspiration and ideas.

And finally, there is, of course, the author's expertise. More than eight years' experience writing interview-winning CVs and cover letters, first through professional CV writing business, Impressive CVs and now via The CV Doctor (www.theCV doctor.co.uk), informs the advice in this book.

In summary, this book incorporates a wealth of knowledge and experience, and will provide you with an excellent insight into how to create your very own impressive CV, cover letter and LinkedIn profile.

Acknowledgements

Shortly after Tom Asker and his team at Little, Brown agreed to publish a second edition of my book, the Coronavrius pandemic struck. Being in lockdown meant I had a lot of time on my hands. Rather than the simple update planned, I was now able to produce a much-improved version that brought the book up to date with latest trends.

By the time this book hits the shelves, I believe the full impact of Covid-19 will be evident and competition in the job market will be at an all-time high. A recent customer shared with me that he applied for a job along with 1,399 other people. Times are tough and it has never been more important to have a CV that 'stands out', a CV that showcases you in the best possible light. My hope is that my book will help you achieve just that!

In short, I would like to thank four sets of people who have contributed to this book. First, senior HR professionals who have provided their viewpoint – their quotes and comments can be found throughout the book. Special thanks to Mark Thomas, Talent Acquisition and Development Director at Abcam (previously Head of Group Resourcing & Talent at Tesco); Sean O'Donoghue, MD at Fifth Gen Recruitment (previously Head of Professional Services at Adecco Group); Anna Tomkins, Head of Talent and Resourcing at Vodafone; Adrian Cojocaru, Director at Tabernam Skinner Ltd (previously MD, Human Resources at EBRD); Daniell Morrisey, Senior Editorial Early Careers Schemes Manager at the BBC and Sean Jowell, Products MD Recruitment Lead for Europe at Accenture. Thank you for your continued support and contributions to this edition.

What makes this book unique is real-life examples. I would like to therefore my customers from both 'The CV Doctor' and 'Impressive

CVs' who kindly granted permission to publish their documents. Personal details and companies they have been affiliated with have been removed to protect their identities. Examples maintained from the first edition have been brought up to date and in line with current trends.

My next thank you goes to my amazing team of freelancers from Impressive CVs days – Linda Baldwin, Sue Bryant, Kay LaRocca, Jo Lamb, Yvette Segal and Katie Slater. Some of your work is featured online which no doubt will add value to those reading this book.

Fourth, I would like to acknowledge fellow CV-writing professionals, Robin Webb and Victoria McLean for their input. Robin, Principal CV Consultant at CV Master Careers, purchased Impressive CVs from me in 2010 after managing the business for 12 months. The business has since amalgamated with CV Master Careers. Robin has extensive experience helping clients at all levels improve their career prospects and also delivers redundancy training to major corporates. Victoria, CEO and founder of City CV, has devoted her career to guiding professionals at all levels with career transition and development. I joined Victoria and her team in 2016 as a Freelance CV Writer and chose to adopt her new style of CV writing as it really was a great way to showcase a candidate's skills and experience.

Most importantly, I would like to thank my husband, Charlie, for his continued support; my two beautiful children, Cade and Erin, who keep me forever on my toes; my parents, Lyn and Laurence and my brother Paul, who have always believed in me; my half-sister, Deborah, who I am so happy to have in my life; and my friends. I love you all dearly.

And, of course, I would like to thank you! Thank you for purchasing my book and for providing me with an opportunity to help. What drives me is helping others and I hope after reading this book, I help you win your dream job.

How to Use this Book

Part One will provide you with an understanding of the job-hunting process from mental preparation right the way through to embracing change.

Once you have identified your target position and bridged any skills gaps, select a template and begin crafting your CV. Part Two will walk you through the process by following a sequence of chapters, each of which is dedicated to a separate section of your CV.

Templates, together with several real-life examples are hosted here: https://www.thecvdoctor.co.uk/how-to-write-an-impressive-cv. Password is: Impr3ss1ve. There is also an appendix at the end of the book with four hundred action words to help create an impactful CV.

Once your CV is complete, proceed to Part Three: Writing a LinkedIn profile. Follow the step-by-step process to create a powerful profile that is keyword searchable. Work hard to build your network and acquire recommendations and endorsements relevant to your career objective.

Then the fun starts. Refer again to Part One for ways to identify job opportunities. When you have identified a role or company that is a good match for your skill set and experience, begin working on your cover letter.

Part Four of the book guides you through the process of creating a tailored, interview-winning cover letter. Refer to the examples hosted on The CV Doctor website (as above) for inspiration.

Before applying for a role, ensure your CV and cover letter are targeted to the role in question and include keywords from the job description and person specification.

Feel free to contact me via my website should you have any questions or feedback.

PART ONE

The Job-hunting Process

CHAPTER 1

How to Approach Job Hunting

Job hunting is defined as the act of looking for employment due to unemployment or discontent with a current position. Job acquisition, if done properly is a full-time job and follows a distinct process:

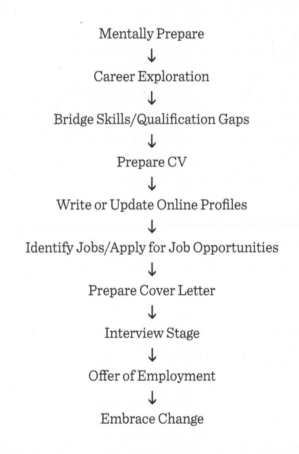

Mentally Prepare
↓
Career Exploration
↓
Bridge Skills/Qualification Gaps
↓
Prepare CV
↓
Write or Update Online Profiles
↓
Identify Jobs/Apply for Job Opportunities
↓
Prepare Cover Letter
↓
Interview Stage
↓
Offer of Employment
↓
Embrace Change

This chapter examines each of these steps. Preparing your CV and cover letters are covered in detail in the next two parts of the book.

STEP 1: Mentally Prepare

The first step to job hunting is to mentally prepare yourself for two things:

1. To open a new chapter in your life.

Changing job should be viewed as a positive, life-changing experience, and you need to focus on how your life will benefit from this change. You will face new challenges, meet new people, learn new things and new ways of doing things. Be prepared to adapt and embrace the possibility of change.

2. For the realities of the job-hunting process.

Finding a job is a job in itself. Devote time, energy and passion to the process and do not be tempted to cut corners. Rather than firing out fifty applications, send out five applications and do them well. Every job application should be a masterpiece, tailored to the job opportunity – you only get one chance to make a first impression.

Job hunting is stressful and it is easy to become despondent. Keep sight of your goal and your employment values. However, in challenging job market conditions, be flexible in your approach, think outside the box and be prepared to consider alternative opportunities.

STEP 2: Career Exploration

The most difficult part of finding a job is often deciding what that job should be. Without a goal in mind it can be difficult if not impossible to realise your dream.

'If you don't know where you are going, how can you expect to get there?'
BASIL S. WALSH

'Without goals and plans to reach them, you are like a ship that has set sail with no destination.'
FITZHUGH DODSON

Before you begin your search, define your employment values and be clear about the kind of position that you are looking to secure.

Answer the following questions about yourself:

- What motivates you?
- What are you passionate about?
- What are your priorities?
- What skills, knowledge and experience do you posses?
- What do you like most/least about your current job?
- What do you want more of; what do you want less of?
- What do you want to change?
- What factors in life are most important to you?

'The first thing to think about is what you enjoy and what you're good at and really be clear in your own head about what type of career you're looking for. Mapping out some sort of a life vision of where you want to go is really important.'

MARK THOMAS, TALENT ACQUISITION AND DEVELOPMENT DIRECTOR AT ABCAM

'Find out what really motivates you and what motivates you is often what you enjoy doing. If you can discover that, your life will be much richer as a result, in all areas.'

GILES CREWDSON, PARTNER AT CREWDSON & PARTNERS

How to determine your target position:

Self-assessment – Examine your answers to each question based on what you know about yourself. What type of role(s) fit your criteria? Identify which companies are a good fit.

Peer/management assessment – Ask people who know you well, on both a professional and personal level, to provide feedback on each area. Also revisit old performance appraisals as these can be very informative.

Self-help methods – Utilise career guidance books or employ the services of a career coach. Consulting with a professional can be very enlightening as they have experience of assessing career options and determining realistic career goals and strategies. They can also help to build or rebuild confidence.

External assessment – Complete standardised tests and exercises that are designed to help you make better career choices. Psychometric testing can be undertaken online, through colleges, universities or through private career counselling services. Another option is to access online job sites: input your core skills into their search criteria and assess the results of possible job matches.

Once you have a target position in mind:

1. Prepare a list of job titles that best describe your talent and which utilise the skills and experience that you have;
2. Identify any skills or qualification gaps;
3. Determine the industry and type of employer you would like to work for.

STEP 3: Bridge Skills or Qualification Gaps

Should you not have all the skills, qualifications or experience required to undertake a particular role, it may be necessary to upskill. Upskilling will improve your employment prospects. This can be achieved in two ways:

1. **Training** – You may need to complete a specific course or qualification.
2. **Gaining experience** – Consider voluntary or part-time work; not only would you gain the necessary experience and some valuable contacts, but also, a useful insight into whether the career you have earmarked is really the right one for you.

STEP 4: Prepare Your CV

This step is covered in detail in Part Two. It covers the importance of having a targeted, well-polished, professional CV and provides step-by-step guidance on how to prepare an interview-winning CV.

STEP 5: Write or Update Online Profile

Professional networking sites like LinkedIn are incredibly popular with employers so ensure you are visible online. This is covered in detail in Part Three of this book.

Platforms like LinkedIn and Twitter can boost your public profile and highlight your skills. Consider a personal website or a Facebook page to showcase your skills and experience. Instagram or a blog are useful in the creative sectors.

It is imperative that your digital footprint is professional and clean. A simple name search on Google will reveal your online presence. Work to remove anything damaging. Double check privacy settings to keep your personal life private

STEP 6: Identify/Apply for Job Opportunities

Once you have prepared your CV, the next step is to begin identifying opportunities and applying for roles. Job-hunting requires a proactive, organised and tenacious approach. Keep a spreadsheet of jobs applications, including the date you applied, contact name, job title, company, follow-up date and outcome.

Below are six ways to identify potential opportunities:

1.   Networking

Effective networking is central to any active job search. There are three areas to concentrate on:

(a) Contacts

Connect with people you know and their respective network. There is your professional network of current and former colleagues, and then your private network made up of friends, family and those people you have met socially at non-work functions. Maintain regular contact with those able to positively impact your job search.

Join groups relevant to your industry or profession and follow inspirational industry professionals.

(b) Networking sites

Join business and social networking sites such as:

- www.linkedin.com
- www.facebook.com
- www.twitter.com
- www.craigslist.org

'Different industries have adopted different social media. In television production, Facebook has grown into the go to location – there's multiple groups covering every role where jobs and opportunities are advertised as well as groups where people post their CVs seeking jobs or freelance work. There are also many talent databases with both free and paid-for memberships. Companies use these to search for candidates. If you use social media, like Twitter, Instagram and Facebook, remember that someone reading your CV might be tempted to take a look – so think about what you post and check your privacy settings.'

DANIELL MORRISEY, SENIOR EDITORIAL EARLY CAREERS SCHEMES MANAGER, AT THE BBC

Many organisations, including headhunting firms and agencies trawl these regularly to identify new talent.

Tip

Potential employers may 'google' candidate names as part of due diligence and reference checking; inappropriate photos/comments on sites like Facebook can be very damaging.

(c) Attend events

Regularly attend careers fairs, seminars and conferences where you are likely to meet new or existing contacts.

Be relentless in your networking activities because the famous saying in business still holds true today, 'it's not what you know it is who you know'.

2. Targeting specific companies

Making a direct approach to a company, whether through a contact or speculatively, can be an excellent way of finding out about opportunities that are not yet in the public domain.

(a) Named contact

If you have been provided with a lead, write to your contact in the first instance, sending them your CV and cover letter. Follow up a week later with a phone call to determine how best to progress your application.

(b) Speculative approach

If you are approaching companies speculatively to see what opportunities may exist for someone with your skills and experience, identify a targeted list of companies that you would like to work for and research each one. Establish who the correct contact would be; in smaller companies aim for the hiring authority or Human Resources Director; in larger organisations, contact the Head of Resourcing or Head of Talent. Follow up with a phone call a week later.

Many companies are very open to receiving applications on spec and as such, this is a very good way of getting your details in front of them. Refer to Part Four for help with writing an effective cover letter.

3. The internet

The internet is a powerful tool to jump-start your job hunt. Not only does it provide you with access to employers' career sites, but it is a research tool that provides you with access to an infinite amount of information on companies, industries, professions and much more.

(a) Targeting specific companies

If you have a specific company in mind, visit their website. Most UK companies use online recruitment as part of their strategy to attract potential candidates. This is a relatively easy way to determine what opportunities are available and may even highlight possibilities you had not previously considered. If there is nothing immediately suitable, some company websites allow you to opt for job alerts via email. As mentioned in point two above, you could always send your CV on a speculative basis.

(b) Job boards/job sites

Job boards are a mainstream part of the recruitment process for jobseekers and for employers or recruiters seeking qualified candidates.

Most job boards allow you to search by keywords, occupation, salary level, preferred geographic location and job type (permanent, part-time, temporary or contract). Different job boards have different qualities and features. Find two/there that best meet your needs.

With some job sites and job boards, once registered, you can opt for job alerts via email. You also have the option of uploading your CV. This makes it easy for you to apply for jobs and for employers or recruiters to access your information.

According to WikiJob, the ten most popular job boards are:

1.   Indeed (www.indeed.co.uk) – For people who don't have the time or patience to search multiple websites.
2.   Total Jobs (www.totaljobs.co.uk) – For those wishing to strengthen their skills and access a high volume of vacancies in one place.
3.   Reed (www.reed.co.uk) – For those looking for jobs at specific companies.
4.   CV Library (www.cv-library.co.uk) – For job-seekers who don't have the time to trawl through results.
5.   Monster (www.monster.co.uk) – For people who prefer to use social media to find and advertise jobs.
6.   Adzuna (www.adzuna.co.uk) – For those who want to know what they are worth.
7.   Glassdoor (www.glassdoor.co.uk) – For those who want to know more about the companies they are applying to work for.
8.   CW Jobs (www.cwjobs.co.uk) – For people seeking a job in technology.
9.   Guardian Jobs (jobs.theguardian.com) – For those looking for high-calibre jobs in specific sectors.

10. Work in Startups (www.workinstartups.com) - For those wanting to work within the UK start-up environment.

It is often worth identifying specialist or niche job boards that are specific to your occupation or industry.

4. Recruitment agencies

Many agencies are reputed for treating you as a number and for providing little or no value to your job search. Albeit, recruitment consultants are a valuable source of information as it is their job to be informed about what is happening in the job market. They have contacts at multiple companies across a range of industries with direct access to many jobs opportunities.

The key is to find the right agent to represent you. Tap into your network for a referral and identify niche agencies that specialise in your industry or sector. Forging a strong relationship with your consultant will shorten your job search.

'A good recruitment agent will have strong knowledge of the job market; they know which employers are hiring and are aware of upcoming positions not yet advertised. They help prepare your CV for selected companies, guide you through the interview process and should you make it to offer stage, they will become your "negotiator" to ensure you receive the best package possible.'
SEAN O'DONOGHUE, MD AT FIFTH GEN RECRUITMENT

When registering with agencies, register with no more than two or three. If a consultant knows you are registered with many agencies, they are likely to allocate less time to you and your job search. Another reason is that agencies may send your CV to clients unsolicited. If you have many agencies representing you, it is possible your CV could end up on someone's desk more than once. This makes you look desperate and over-exposed in the market.

> *'Candidates only need one or two good consultancies that can represent them to the companies they want to work for. There is no benefit having one's CV registered with ten different agencies – candidates will lose track of where their CV has gone and it can become very embarrassing.'*
>
> SEAN O'DONOGHUE MD AT FIFTH GEN RECRUITMENT

5. Headhunters/executive search firms

For candidates seeking senior or executive roles it is well worth approaching a select number of executive search firms who specialise in your industry or sector. Headhunters operate at the top end of the market and are often retained by blue-chip organisations to tap into the market and secure top talent. Most headhunting firms are open to receiving CVs on a speculative basis but you need to be aware that unless they have an opening for you at this moment in time, you are likely to be placed on to their database and will only be contacted should something suitable come up in the future. Search firms are focused primarily on fulfilling their clients' needs and as such, they will not spend time searching out a role for you. If, however, they see potential or if your skillset is in demand, they may discuss your credentials with key clients.

6. Newspapers and trade publications

Although online postings are a more common form of advertising, many companies still continue to place advertisements in the local/national press and in trade publications, so this can be another good source of jobs.

Tip

Be proactive and relentless in your job search. Try a combination of methods and be sure to have a 'few irons in the fire'. Aim to apply for up to five roles each week.

STEP 7: Prepare Your Cover Letter

Part Four covers this topic in detail, from the importance of including a cover letter with your application, through to how to prepare an interview-winning letter for a specific role and on spec.

STEP 8: Interview Stage

If you have a well-written, targeted CV and cover letter, and you are a good match for the role, you are likely to be short-listed and contacted for interview.

Should you be invited to interview, email the interviewer straight after the meeting to thank them for their time and explain how much you enjoyed meeting with them. This will make you stand out and be remembered.

Should you not hear from the agency or company after the closing date, contact the employer or recruitment professional to enquire about the status of your application. If you are not invited to interview or if you are rejected at interview stage, obtain feedback as you can build on this.

STEP 9: Job Offer

Should you be offered the role, thank the person. Ensure you are satisfied with the terms of employment. This is the time to negotiate or iron out any concerns.

If you are currently employed, ensure you have a signed offer of employment before handing in your resignation.

STEP 10: Embrace Change

If you have elected to accept the offer, you will be feeling one of two things: excitement or fear; perhaps a combination of both. Both these emotions are totally normal.

'I'm not afraid of storms, for I'm learning to sail my ship.'
LOUISA MAY ALCOTT

Change is the law of life. If we look at this in the context of the recruitment industry, individuals that change jobs every few years are likely to develop and progress their careers more quickly than those who stay put. People that become comfortable and complacent cannot grow as they are not stretching themselves or the boundaries. People often resist change because they are scared of failure. Unless you keep abreast of change, your skills can lose their edge and even become obsolete. Often change involves adapting your style, your thought pattern and being willing to learn and accept new ways of doing things.

'I think new challenges are good and if you can go into different organisations, take away their best practices and then come into another organisation and share those best practises, I think it's great.'
BINDU SUDRA, SENIOR MANAGER, TALENT MANAGEMENT AND PERFORMANCE LEADER AT KPMG

For companies, it is important to constantly have fresh talent joining them as this brings new ideas and innovative ways of thinking to their organisation.

'There's a lot more movement than there used to be. It's seen to be a very healthy thing.'
WILL DAWKINS, PARTNER AT SPENCER STUART

Change can be scary but it is how we grow.

Continue to the next chapter for some important job-hunting tips.

CHAPTER 2

Job-hunting Tips

Below are some important tips that will help you through the whole job acquisition process:

1. Identify your career goals
Where are you going and what do you need to do to get there?

2. Plan
Job hunting is a full-time job; structure your day with specific tasks and goals.

3. Keep your search targeted
Rather than carpet bomb the market with several applications, identify roles that are a strong match to your skill set. Tailor your CV and cover letter for each application as this will increase your odds significantly.

4. Research your industry
Do your homework and identify companies that you may want to work for.

5. Be flexible
In a competitive environment, it may be necessary to compromise on certain aspects of the job, for example, suitability, level, location, or salary.

6. Be organised and record everything you do
Keep a log of all job applications including dates, contact details, company name, follow-up date and outcome.

'It needs to be a planned activity and what's really important is keeping records of what you've sent to whom, so when people start contacting you have a record of everything.'
ANNA TOMKINS, HEAD OF TALENT AND RESOURCING AT VODAFONE

7. Check your social media footprint

Ensure you have a strong LinkedIn profile and that your social media footprint is professional.

8. Become interview fit

Attend all interviews. It builds confidence and it is a good learning experience.

9. Prepare for each interview

Establish the likely structure of each interview and prepare accordingly. Thoroughly research the company, the interviewee and the role prior to interview. Practice likely questions and answers. Show enthusiasm for the company and the role throughout the process.

10. Get feedback

If unsuccessful at CV or interview stage, ask for feedback. This can be invaluable for future applications.

11. Remain motivated

Job-hunting is time consuming and emotionally draining. It is natural and easy to lapse into a negative spiral and be tempted just to give up when things are taking longer than expected. Stay focused, keep positive, and be patient. Good things come to those that wait.

'You need to have realistic expectations; it can take time regardless of the role, your level or what you're looking for.'
ANNA TOMKINS , HEAD OF TALENT AND RESOURCING AT VODAFONE

12. Stay marketable

Expand on skills and knowledge every six to 12 months. Update your CV and LinkedIn profile every six months. More on this in the following chapter.

'The difference between a successful person and others is not a lack of strength, not a lack of knowledge, but rather in a lack of will.'

VINCENT T. LOMBARDI

CHAPTER 3

Staying Marketable

Once you have secured your new job, it is important to actively manage your own career. The job for life culture is a thing of the past; nowadays, it is up to you to invest in your future. This is increasingly important in a competitive environment.

Job security comes from within and is your ability to find a job rapidly should the need arise. You need to invest time and effort into staying marketable so you can respond quickly to tight market conditions or to a new opportunity.

To progress and stay ahead of the competition, you need to:

1. **Stay abreast of changes in your industry and market** – Read relevant industry magazines, and attend seminars and conferences regularly;
2. **Keep your network alive** – Consistently build and maintain your professional network; this is crucial to your ongoing marketability. It keeps you abreast of new opportunities and of changes in or outside your area of expertise;
3. **Professional development/upskill** – Complete industry specific qualifications and courses, whether external or internal;
4. **Update your CV twice a year** – This helps you remember what you have done or achieved. It makes life much easier should an amazing opportunity arise.

It is easy to become stuck in a rut – it is comfortable, but don't do it!

PART TWO

CV Writing

CHAPTER 4

You Had Better Get it Right!

To appeal to prospective employers, you need a targeted, well-polished, professional CV that differentiates you from the crowd. A CV is your 'marketing tool' and the way you present yourself to a prospective employer can be the difference between being invited to interview and your CV being binned. The next chapters will take you through a step-by-step process of putting together an interview-winning CV. Before we begin, let's discuss exactly what a CV is, why it is so important to get it right, what the experts have to say, understanding ATS and the importance of keeping it truthful.

What is a CV?

A Curriculum Vitae is Latin for '*the course of one's life*' and is defined by the Collins Dictionary as, '*an outline of a person's educational and professional history, usually prepared for job applications*'.

The Importance of Getting it Right

When applying for a job, regardless of profession, you will usually be required to provide your CV. A CV is used to help a prospective employer determine your fit for the role and is your first communication with the prospective employer. As you are often competing against hundreds of applicants, your CV needs to stand out in terms of both layout and content. To compromise on the quality of your CV will only compromise your chances of securing an interview.

Recruitment professionals are often the first point of entry, so they are the people you need to impress.

They often use an Applicant Tracking System (ATS) to sort through candidates as they do not have the time to sift through what is often hundreds of applications. ATS also provides an organised system to keep track of applications.

Understanding the Importance of ATS

If you are serious about finding a job, it is vital to understand how an ATS works, otherwise you risk creating a fantastic CV that no one will ever read.

What is ATS?

ATS is a popular tool used by recruiters to sort and filter candidates in order of suitability for a role based on essential skills and experience. Recruiters identify candidates by inputting keywords to find candidates that match set criteria.

How Does it Work?

The system searches all candidate CVs for relevant keywords. The ATS looks for keywords in different sections of the CV, for example, 'Profile', 'Key Skills' and 'Employment History'. The ATS will then calculate which of the CVs contain the highest density of relevant keywords and displays a list of the CVs which best meet the recruiters desired criteria. The system will usually automatically filter out and discard CVs that do not have sufficient keyword density. This means if your CV does not match, it is unlikely to make it through the electronic sift and will never be read by a human recruiter.

How Important is ATS to Employers?

This one is best answered by employers. All three that I spoke to concurred that we do need to be mindful of ATS when creating our CV.

Talent Acquisition and Development Director at Abcam (previously Head of Group Resourcing and Talent at Tesco), Mark Thomas, commented that, 'ATS is important for aspects such as candidate relationship management, interview scheduling, microsites, referrals or reporting, but they are not an adequate substitute for proper talent scouting. The days of 'post and pray' are long gone and companies are increasingly focusing on quality of hire and sourcing passive as well as active candidates.'

Anna Tomkins, Head of Talent and Resourcing at Vodafone, stated that Vodafone do have an ATS system, and yes, it is important. She said, 'We typically receive 100,000 applications a year in the UK, so it's really important to us to understand who has applied and what to.'

Senior Editorial Early Careers Schemes Manager at the BBC, Daniell Morrissey, had this to say: 'Recruitment companies and many employers use an ATS as the platform through which you apply for roles or to upload your CV into a talent database, which they then match to roles or freelance opportunities. Most systems scan your CV and abstract words to fields in a database. Users of the system likewise use words to search the database and find relevant candidates. It's therefore crucial that you include everything you want to be searched against in your CV – technical and soft skills and specialist knowledge.'

Getting your CV through ATS filtering

Your CV needs to be optimised for ATS algorithms. Robin Webb, Principal CV Consultant at CV Master Careers, has this advice: 'The best approach is to match keywords in your CV to keywords mentioned in the job description/advert for a specific role you are targeting. If you are making lots of applications, you should review a range of relevant job adverts and try to pick out which keywords will be most important. For best results, ensure you include the keywords in all relevant sections of your CV (such as your profile, key skills and employment history). I would not recommend using 'word-clouds' as these could be viewed as cheating. You also need to ensure the CV still reads well and makes sense to the human reader once it has made it through the sift.'

Top tips to tailor your CV for ATS:
- Include keywords and phrases that mirror those in the job description/specification. For example, if the role mentions that you need good customer service skills, don't refer to

yourself as client-focused. It is fine to use synonyms but do mention the exact word or phrase at least one.

- Use simple, professional looking fonts – see Chapter 18.
- Label sections with standard headings like Employment History and Education.
- Chronological CVs are the most ATS-friendly.
- Specify qualifications by name.
- Keep formatting simple.
- Use bullet points.
- Avoid fancy fonts and logos.

When optimising your CV for the ATS, don't lose sight of the recruiter and employer, because when your CV passes the test it still needs to look good visually and read well.

Tip

There are online ATS checkers that you can use to determine how well your CV scores in relation to the job being applied for.

What the Experts Say about the Current State of CVs

Candidates often underestimate the importance of a CV and do a rushed, inadequate job. Below are the views of our experts:

'CVs are hit and miss. We end up having to modify 50% of the CVs we receive.'
SEAN O'DONOGHUE, MD AT FIFTH GEN RECRUITMENT

'There has been an marked improvement in the quality of CVs over the past few years, especially regarding format and layout, which makes it easier for recruiters to identify skill and behaviours.'
SEAN JOWELL, PRODUCTS MD RECRUITMENT LEAD FOR EUROPE AT ACCENTURE

'Very bad'
MARK THOMAS, TALENT ACQUISITION AND DEVELOPMENT DIRECTOR AT ABCAM

'Many CVs I see are unfocused – think of the advert or job description as the problem and your CV as the solution. If it's not focused, then it's not clear what you're offering and whether you're the answer to their question. CVs are your brochure, so make yours commercial and scannable and think carefully about the layout and design. People are still stuck with old fashioned templates and include unnecessary detail.'
DANIELL MORRISEY, SENIOR EDITORIAL EARLY CAREERS SCHEMES MANAGER
AT THE BBC

Stretching the truth

CVs need to be factual. Do not be tempted to stretch the truth or tell half- truths. Minor embellishments or lying can be the worst mistake you can make on your CV.

'If you say you had an MA when it was a BA, or you went to Business School without pointing out the fact that you didn't graduate, that looks to the client as if you're lying. It's not really a lie, it's sort of a half-truth isn't it but the impact on your reputation is terrible. If you get caught doing it once, it sticks.'
WILL DAWKINS, PARTNER AT SPENCER STEWART

'Most large companies these days undertake various forms of background checking between the point when somebody is offered a job and when they actually start. Part of this will indeed include validating that what you have represented on your CV is correct – so it's very important to make sure that it's all watertight and above board.'
JONATHAN JONES, HEAD OF TALENT AT ROIVANT PHARMA

Conclusion

In a market that is becoming more and more competitive, it has never been more important to have a first-class, optimised and factual CV. A step-by-step process of how to achieve this is covered in the subsequent chapters. With each step you take, you are one step closer to securing your dream job.

CHAPTER 5

Determining the Most Suitable CV Type

In order to grab the reader's attention and increase your chances of being invited to interview, you need to have a CV that will best showcase your skills and experience.

The three CV types – chronological, skills-based/functional and hybrid/combined CVs – are defined and discussed next.

Chronological CV

Defined

The definition of *chronology* as defined by the Collins dictionary is *'the determination of the proper sequence of events'*.

As the definition suggests, a chronological CV provides a detailed account of your career and educational history in order. The information needs to be presented in reverse chronological order, i.e. most recent information first.

When to use a chronological CV
- You have a solid career history in a particular field, industry or discipline.
- You have no major time gaps between positions.
- You have worked for well-known companies with good reputations and have held impressive job titles.
- You are looking to highlight your most recent jobs.
- You have clearly defined career goals.

Advantages of a chronological CV
- A chronological CV is considered to be the traditional approach

and is the most commonly used CV type.

- Easy for the reader to follow.

'If it comes in a chronological order, to me that's a complete jigsaw that you've built and I can see it, but that is a personal style preference.'

ANNA TOMKINS, HEAD OF TALENT AND RESOURCING AT VODAFONE

Example of a chronological CV

Melissa Stewart
LU7 | +44 1234 567 890 | melstewart@abcd.co.uk

TEAM LEADER

Professional, ambitious **Senior Flight Attendant with over eight years' commercial experience** within a variety of roles including airline cabin crew, PR, & document management. Extensive team leadership experience having recruited, mentored, and managed teams of up to eight staff. Now seeking a role as a Team Leader in a customer-focused environment.

Career Highlights:
- ✓ Represented company at various prestigious events, including press and media meetings for new product launches and rugby sporting events.
- ✓ Consistently achieved monthly targets for onboard Duty-Free-Sales; receives regular awards and management recognition.
- ✓ Streamlined company processes and procedures; eliminated backlog and improved efficiency.

KEY SKILLS

- Customer Service
- Relationship Management
- Sales / Business Development
- Process Improvement
- Team Leadership

- Problem Solving
- Multi-Lingual
- Presentation Skills
- IT Skills
- Public Relations

CAREER HISTORY

Senior Flight Attendant: CAT Airline, Hayes   Aug'XX–Present
Recruited to provide a quality service to first-class business travellers, supply silver service to customers and assist cockpit crew. Supervises eight junior cabin crew members responsible for passenger load of 300.

- **Effectively managed an emergency landing situation;** utilised fire-fighting skills during an incident over the Atlantic en route to New York.
- **Escorted British Civil Aviation Authorities on selected aircraft test routes** as an ambassador for TGA Airlines, when purchasing new aircraft.
- Consistently react quickly and calmly to diffuse and prevent escalation of customer complaints or difficult behaviour.
- **Active role model** in the training of junior cabin crew in safety and security procedures.

Senior Flight Supervisor: GA Airlines Airways, London   Sep'XX–Aug'XX
Joined as a Junior member of the cabin crew, progressing to a senior role after two years, supervising a team of four junior members.

- **Selected to attend several high-profile client events;** attended to clients' needs in a discreet and confidential manner.
- **Consistently commended by clients and management** for providing exemplary levels of customer care.
- **Mentored and trained junior cabin crew;** two of which were promoted within twelve months.

PR Representative: BRR Associates, Bournemouth   Sept'XX–Aug'XX
Secured part-time position representing blue-chip companies at PR events. Provided information to the general-public and applied skills of persuasion to achieve promotional sales targets.
- **Secured over 700 new customer contract signings during a single 12-hour shift against target of 300, for their Phones4U client.**

Microfilm Supervisor: ABC Bank plc, Surrey   Sept'XX–Aug'XX
Hired to oversee and manage the input of sensitive documentation.
- **Re-organised the daily flow of documents into the office using an improved design system;** interviewed, selected, and trained a team of five staff to manage the system.
- **Headed monthly corporate presentations and conferences** on business productivity and profit to an audience of senior/regional managers from all UK offices.
- **Streamlined the organisation of the microfilm division;** re-evaluated an eight-month backlog within a period of just two months.

EARLY CAREER

Hair Stylist and Colour Technician in the UK

EDUCATION AND TRAINING

CBC & Group Classes in Management, CAT College, Hayes, 20XX–20XX
Modules included: Motivating teams, Assertiveness, Business Writing, Problem Solving, Providing Feedback, Coaching, Managing Difficult People, Superior Customer Service, Leading the Way and Resolving Conflict.

Ecology Diploma, The British School of Yoga, 20XX
World Religion Diploma, The British School of Yoga, 20XX
IATA Airline Marketing Diploma, CAT College, Hayes, 20XX
City & Guilds NVQ 1,2 & 3 Hair & Beauty, Kingston College, Surrey, 19XX–19XX

VOLUNTARY WORK

- **24-hour member of the Worldwide Emergency Assistance Team**, specialising in critical aviation emergencies
- **Provided administration skills for ABC charity**, which achieved its registration as an official charity in the UK in October 20XX
- **Teacher's Assistant at ACA Special Needs** school during 20XX
- **Volunteered at RCA Rehabilitation Centre** in the UK for children recovering from major accidents from 20XX to 20XX
- **Completed a sponsored skydive** to raise funds for the National Asthma Campaign and Multiple Sclerosis organisations in 20XX

- It is the preferred choice of most recruitment professionals and the most widely recognised.
- It is a good way of showing progression and growth.
- It compliments a continuous career history within the same discipline.

Skills-based/Functional CV

Defined
As the name suggests, a skills-based or functional CV is focused on transferable skills rather than chronological work history.

When to use a functional CV
- You are changing career or work direction into a different field, industry or discipline.
- You are applying for a job where you have little or no previous relevant experience.
- You have a chequered work history or have been in one job or industry for a very long time.
- You do not have direct experience to the role to which you are applying.
- You have significant gaps in your career.
- You have held several very similar positions.
- You are looking to downsize or take a step back.
- You want to emphasise work or achievements from your early career.
- You have been recently absent from the job market.
- You have had several very different jobs or have frequently changed employer.

Advantages of a functional CV
- It accentuates your transferable skills.
- It enables you to detract attention away from your career history.

Example of a Skills-based/Functional CV

Melissa Stewart

LU7 | +44 1234 567 890 | melstewart@abcd.co.uk

TEAM LEADER

Professional, ambitious **Senior Flight Attendant with over eight years' commercial experience** within a variety of roles including airline cabin crew, PR, & document management. Extensive team leadership experience recruited, mentored, and managed teams of up to eight staff.
Now seeking a role as a Team Leader in a customer-focused environment.

CAREER HIGHLIGHTS

- ✓ Represented company at various prestigious events, including press and media meetings for new product launches and rugby sporting events.
- ✓ Played an active role in effectively managing an emergency landing situation; utilised fire-fighting skills during an incident over the Atlantic en route to New York.
- ✓ Escorted British Civil Aviation Authorities on selected aircraft test routes as an ambassador for TGA Airlines, when purchasing new aircraft.
- ✓ Secured over 700 new customer contract signings during a single 12-hour shift, against a target of 300, for their Phones4U client.
- ✓ Consistently achieved monthly targets for onboard Duty-Free-Sales; receives regular awards and management recognition.
- ✓ Streamlined company processes and procedures; eliminated backlog and improved efficiency.

KEY SKILLS

Communication / Language Skills
- Possesses excellent interpersonal skills, highly perceptive and quickly able to develop relationships with customers and colleagues.
- Headed monthly corporate presentations and conferences on business productivity and profit to an audience of senior/regional managers from all UK offices.
- Conversational French; currently learning Arabic with basic skills in sign language.

Customer Service
- Skilled with interpreting individual requirements and providing an empathetic approach.
- Provides a high quality of service to First Class Business travellers; ensure their safety, entertainment and catering requirements are all managed efficiently.
- Reacts quickly and calmly to diffuse and prevent escalation of potential customer complaints or difficult behaviour.
- Attends to the needs of many high-profile clients in a discreet and confidential manner.

Leadership and Training
- Proven ability to create and maintain a positive and motivational environment for both customers and staff alike.
- Experienced with supervising teams of up to eight cabin crew, with a passenger load of circa 300 customers
- Selected as an active role model in the training of junior cabin crew in safety and security procedures.
- Interviewed, selected, and trained a team of five staff to manage and organise the daily flow of documents into the office using an improved design system.

Problem Solving / Organising
- Applies initiative and creativity to resolve difficult situations; utilises limited resources to compensate for any technical or personal problems experienced by customers.
- Plans, prioritises, and schedules tasks efficiently, maintaining objectivity in difficult situations and handling multiple demands and competing priorities.

CAREER HISTORY

Senior Flight Attendant: CAT Airline, Hayes	Aug XXXX – Date
Senior Flight Supervisor: GA Airlines Airways, London	Sep XXXX – Aug XXXX
PR Representative: BRR Associates, Bournemouth	Sep XXXX – Aug XXXX
Microfilm Supervisor: ABC Bank plc, Surrey	Sep XXXX – Aug XXXX
Hair Stylist and Colour Technician	May XXXX – Sep XXXX

EDUCATION AND TRAINING

CBC & Group Classes in Management, CAT College, Hayes, 20XX
Modules included: Motivating teams, Assertiveness, Business Writing, Problem Solving, Providing Feedback, Coaching, Managing Difficult People, Superior Customer Service, Leading the Way and Resolving Conflict.

Ecology Diploma, The British School of Yoga, 20XX
World Religion Diploma, The British School of Yoga, 20XX
IATA Airline Marketing Diploma, CAT College, Hayes, 20XX
City & Guilds NVQ 1,2 & 3 Hair & Beauty, Kingston College, Surrey, 19XX

VOLUNTARY WORK

- **24-hour member of the Worldwide Emergency Assistance Team**, specialising in critical aviation emergencies
- **Provided administration skills for ABC charity**, which achieved its registration as an official charity in the UK in October 20XX
- **Teacher's Assistant at ACA Special Needs** school during 20XX
- **Volunteered at RCA Rehabilitation Centre** in the UK for children recovering from major accidents from 20XX to 20XX
- **Completed a sponsored skydive** to raise funds for the National Asthma Campaign and Multiple Sclerosis organisations in 20XX

Skills-based CVs do unfortunately raise red flags so where possible opt for a more traditional format. Victoria at City CV had this to say:

'Skills-based/functional CVs just don't work in reality. They confuse the ATS and the recruiter. Avoid them at all costs.'
VICTORIA MCLEAN, CEO AT CITY CV

Hybrid/Combined CV

A hybrid CV combines elements of both chronological and skills-based CVs to include a combination of skills, career and educational history, but in less detail.

When to use a hybrid/combined CV

- You are starting out in the workforce for the first time, changing careers or re-entering the workforce
- You have been in one job or industry for a very long time.
- You are applying for a job where you have little or no previous relevant experience but have an impressive career that you do not want to hide.
- You do not have direct experience in the role you are applying for.
- You have held several very similar positions.

Advantages of a hybrid/combined CV

- You are able to highlight both your transferable skills, accomplishments and your career history.
- The top-loaded style shows recruitment managers the most valuable information.
- The format appeals to traditional and non-traditional recruitment managers.
- The pressure of having career gaps is reduced
- You are still able to show progression and growth.

Example of a hybrid/combined CV

Melissa Stewart

LU7 | +44 1234 567 890 | melstewart@abcd.co.uk

TEAM LEADER

Professional, ambitious **Senior Flight Attendant with over eight years' commercial experience** within a variety of roles including airline cabin crew, PR, & document management. Extensive team leadership experience recruited, mentored, and managed teams of up to eight staff. Seeking Team Leader role in a customer-focused environment.

CAREER HIGHLIGHTS

✓ Represented company at various prestigious events, including press and media meetings for new product launches and rugby sporting events.
✓ Played an active role in managing an emergency landing situation; utilised fire-fighting skills during an incident over the Atlantic en route to New York.
✓ Escorted British Civil Aviation Authorities on selected aircraft test routes as an ambassador for TGA Airlines, when purchasing new aircraft.
✓ Secured over 700 new customer contract signings during a single 12-hour shift, against a target of 300, for their Phones4U client.
✓ Consistently achieved monthly targets for onboard Duty-Free-Sales; receives regular awards and management recognition.
✓ Streamlined company processes and procedures; eliminated backlog and improved efficiency.

KEY SKILLS

Communication / Language Skills
- Possesses excellent interpersonal skills, highly perceptive and quickly able to develop relationships with customers and colleagues.
- Headed monthly corporate presentations and conferences on business productivity and profit to senior/regional managers from all UK offices.
- Conversational French; currently learning Arabic with basic skills in sign language.

Customer Service
- Interprets individual requirements and provides an empathetic approach.
- Provides high quality service to First Class Business travellers; ensure their safety, entertainment and catering requirements are all managed efficiently.
- Reacts quickly to diffuse and prevent escalation of potential customer complaints.
- Attends to needs of high-profile clients in a discreet and confidential manner.

Leadership and Training
- Proven ability to create and maintain a positive and motivational environment for both customers and staff alike.
- Experienced with supervising teams of up to eight cabin crew, with a passenger load of circa 300 customers
- Selected as an active role model in the training of junior cabin crew in safety and security procedures.
- Interviewed, selected, and trained a team of five staff to manage and organise the daily flow of documents into the office using an improved design system.

Problem Solving / Organising
- Applies initiative and creativity to resolve difficult situations; utilises limited resources to compensate for any technical or personal problems experienced by customers.
- Plans, prioritises, and schedules tasks efficiently, maintaining objectivity in difficult situations and handling multiple demands and competing priorities.

CAREER HISTORY

Senior Flight Attendant: CAT Airline, Hayes   Aug'XX–Present
Recruited to provide a quality service to first-class business travellers, supply silver service to customers and assist cockpit crew. Supervises eight junior cabin crew members responsible for passenger load of 300.

- **Effectively managed an emergency landing situation;** utilised fire-fighting skills during an incident over the Atlantic en route to New York.
- **Escorted British Civil Aviation Authorities on selected aircraft test routes** as an ambassador for TGA Airlines, when purchasing new aircraft.
- Consistently react quickly and calmly to diffuse and prevent escalation of customer complaints or difficult behaviour.
- **Active role model** in training junior cabin crew in safety and security procedures.

Senior Flight Supervisor: GA Airlines Airways, London   Sep'XX–Aug'XX
Joined as a Junior member of the cabin crew, progressing to a senior role after two years, supervising a team of four junior members.

- **Selected to attend several high-profile client events;** attended to clients' needs in a discreet and confidential manner.
- **Consistently commended by clients and management** for providing exemplary levels customer care.
- **Mentored and trained junior cabin crew;** two of which were promoted within 12 months.

PR Representative: BRR Associates, Bournemouth   Sept'XX–Aug'XX
Secured part-time position representing blue-chip companies at PR events.

- **Secured over 700 new customer contract signings during a single 12-hour shift** against target of 300, for their Phones4U client.
- **Achieved promotional sales targets;** provided information to general-public.

Microfilm Supervisor: ABC Bank plc, Surrey   Sept'XX–Aug'XX
Hired to oversee and manage the input of sensitive documentation.

- **Re-organised the daily flow of documents into the office using an improved design system;** interviewed, selected, and trained a team of five staff to manage the system.
- **Headed monthly corporate presentations and conferences** on business productivity and profit to an audience of senior/regional managers from all UK offices.
- **Streamlined the organisation of the microfilm division;** re-evaluated an eight-month backlog within a period of just two months.

EDUCATION AND TRAINING

CBC & Group Classes in Management, CAT College, Hayes, 20XX–20XX
Modules included: Motivating teams, Assertiveness, Business Writing, Problem Solving, Providing Feedback, Coaching, Managing Difficult People, Superior Customer Service, Leading the Way and Resolving Conflict.

Ecology Diploma, The British School of Yoga, 20XX
World Religion Diploma, The British School of Yoga, 20XX
IATA Airline Marketing Diploma, CAT College, Hayes, 20XX
City & Guilds NVQ 1,2 & 3 Hair & Beauty, Kingston College, Surrey, 19XX–19XX

VOLUNTARY WORK

- **24-hour member of the Worldwide Emergency Assistance Team**
- **Helped ABC charity** achieve registration as an official UK charity in October 20XX
- **Teacher's Assistant at ACA Special Needs** school during 20XX
- **Volunteered at RCA Rehabilitation Centre** in the UK for children recovering from major accidents from 20XX to 20XX
- **Completed a sponsored skydive** to raise funds for the National Asthma Campaign and Multiple Sclerosis organisations in 20XX

The CV Types Compared

Choosing the right CV type will dramatically increase your chance of being selected for interview. Most job hunters select a chronological or hybrid CV as they are more traditional but sometimes, a skills-led CV, although unconventional, may be a better option to showcase your skills and experience. Do not discount its value. Here are some thoughts from a few of our experts about skills-led/functional CVs:

'I do think they have their place. From a personal preference point of view, my key principle is that past performance predicts future performance. The essence of a CV for me is about key achievements rather than necessarily skills that led to those achievements.'

MARK THOMAS, TALENT ACQUISITION AND DEVELOPMENT DIRECTOR AT ABCAM

'A skills-led CV is entirely appropriate for some roles – healthcare professionals, project managers or professional interims, for example.'

ANNA TOMKINS, HEAD OF TALENT AND RESOURCING AT VODAFONE

'If a candidate is confident they can do the job but they do not have the exact work experience the employer is looking for, they can consider a functional CV.'

SEAN O'DONOGHUE, MD AT FIFTH GEN RECRUITMENT

CHAPTER 6

Heading your CV

Once you have decided on the CV type, select a template and make a start on your CV. Templates are hosted on www.theCVdoctor.co.uk (see 'How to use this Book' for details).

Head your CV with your name, contact information and headline/job title.

1. Your name
- Include your first and last name only.
- Include your qualification alongside your name in smaller font, if it is relevant to the role being applied for.
- Your name will form the focal point of your CV, either on the left-hand side or middle of your page in font size 18 or 20.

2. Contact information
On the same line or beneath your name, provide contact details, including your postcode, email address and contact number. Provide a link to your LinkedIn Profile, video CV, personal website, or blog (if relevant).

'It's critical to have your LinkedIn on your CV, right at the top near your contact information. It points your audience to your online brand and gives them a great snapshot of the real you.'
VICTORIA MCLEAN, CEO AT CITY CV

---

3. Headline/job title
Your job title must be strong, specific and relevant to the role being applied for.

For example: if you are a finance manager seeking a similar role, your headline could be 'Head of Finance', 'Financial Controller' or 'Finance Professional'. Review job boards to see which title produces more matches.

What to Exclude

People are often enticed into adding titles, logos, work contacts and photographs. The reason why each of these should not be included is discussed below.

1. Titles

Do not be tempted to include a title on your CV such as: 'Curriculum Vitae', 'CV' or 'Resume'. It should be obvious what the document is.

2. Logos

Avoid inserting company or other logos; they take up valuable space, cause formatting problems and may interfere with ATS software.

3. Work contact details

Avoid including your work telephone number or email address unless you have very good reason to do so. The consequence could be your employer gets wind of the fact that you are looking to move.

4. Photographs

The trend today is against photographs; they take up a lot of space and they say nothing about your ability to do the job.

Some of the experts interviewed believed that including a photograph was one of the biggest mistakes you could make on your CV:

'Unless you've specifically been asked to provide a photograph in your CV, steer away from it.'

ANNA TOMKINS, HEAD OF TALENT AND RESOURCING AT VODAFONE

'Most UK job seekers do not include photographs in their CV; it is a common practice in Europe and the US. If candidates do include a photograph, they need to ensure that they are professional headshots and not social photos.'

SEAN JOWELL, PRODUCTS MD RECRUITMENT LEAD FOR EUROPE AT ACCENTURE

Tip

Be sure to head the second and each subsequent page of your CV with your name and most appropriate contact number. Should your CV be received or distributed as a hardcopy, it is possible that the pages can become separated.

CHAPTER 7

Personal Profile

Directly after your heading is your personal profile or statement. This offers a snapshot of your skills, experience, background and achievements. It is one of the more time-consuming areas to write as it requires a lot of soul searching to determine who and what you are, what will make you stand out and what accomplishments are worthy of mention. It is, however, an invaluable opportunity to 'sell' yourself and hook the reader's interest.

'I think a profile statement at the top of a CV as a brief summary which sums up the essence of that person can be quite helpful as it can be compelling to the reader. It can create greater interest, it can make you stand out and differentiate you from others.'

MARK THOMAS, TALENT ACQUISITION AND DEVELOPMENT DIRECTOR AT ABCAM

As this is likely to be the first section a hiring authority or recruitment agent will read and you have on average seven seconds to impress your reader, there is quite a lot of pressure to get this section right. Take your time, follow the steps below and I am confident you will create your very own masterpiece.

Steps to Writing your Profile

This section is split into those with less and those with more than two years of experience.

Those with Less Than Two years' Experience:
Step 1: Overview
- Select two personal attributes from page 46 that best describe you.
- Summarise in two/three bullet points your education, experience, passions and any major accomplishments during school, college, or university.

Example 1:
- Self-motivated, committed Economics graduate pursing a master's in Banking and Finance.
- Seasoned private investor with a strong knowledge of financial markets and risk gained during internships with a Fund Manager and large Investment Bank.
- Winner and runner-up in several financial related competitions at University including the National Investment Competition.

Example 2:
- Creative and head-strong fashion undergraduate with an entrepreneurial spirit and a strong work ethic having worked since the age of 14. Now seeking to secure a role as a Fashion Stylist.
- Solid understanding of the history of fashion having regularly attended fashion week in London and Paris and several Vogue Festivals.
- Secured voluntary role at Liberty, shadowing Head Stylist for several weeks; secured a place at their Style Academy, a course usually reserved for full-time employees.

Example 3:
- Career driven, well-organised graduate with a master's degree in Insurance and Risk Management.
- Developed a solid understanding of Risk Management methods during studies and internship at Lloyds Bank with a strong focus on various methods of controlling and identifying risk.

- Displays well-defined analytical and numerical skills as demonstrated by first class Mathematical degree and strong A Level results in Core Pure Maths & Statistics.

Example 4:

- Creative and innovative graduate with an Honours Degree in Product Design from Bath University.
- Passionate about product design and project management with a talent for problem solving and the analytical side of design process.
- Devised two market ready products at University from planning, research and analysis, through to design, prototype and product launch.

Step 2: Career Objective

For entry-level job seekers and graduates, it is helpful to the reader if you detail what type of role you are looking for – be specific not vague. Rather than say, 'seeking an exciting role in a fast-paced work environment where I can utilise my skills and experience gained at university', rather state, 'seeking to secure a role as a Junior Developer' or 'seeking a role as a Trainee Analyst'. This can be included as part of a bullet or as a Headline just above your profile statement.

Those with More Than Two Years' Experience:

Step 1: Overview

- Select two personal attributes from page 46 that best describe you.
- Summarise in two sentences what you have done, for how long, your focus or area of expertise and what industry or sector you have worked in. If applicable, mention qualifications or academic achievements and companies you have worked with or for.

Example 1:
Driven and highly self-motivated IT Project Manager with more than

twenty years of experience providing strategic IT solutions to a variety of key sectors across Europe, including government departments. Excellent technical project management skills with detailed exposure to project planning, risk management, issue management, configuration management, progress reporting and software quality assurance.

Example 2:
Passionate, adaptable teaching assistant with seven years' teaching experience across KS1 and KS2. Engages easily with children and possesses an innate ability to adjust teaching style to suit age group. Educated to degree level with a Level 3 Teaching Assistant's Diploma.

Example 3:
Highly analytical and self-motivated engineer with a PhD in Mechanical Engineering and extensive experience of planning and managing several high-level research projects. Expert in rotational moulding and polymer processing with a demonstrable record of using statistical analysis, mathematical modelling and computer simulation to improve and develop company processes.

Example 4:
Artistic and innovative architect with strong design skills, time-cased management and ten years' experience in architecture and the built environment. Managed multi-disciplinary, international architectural projects at the forefront of global construction including energy-saving trends and unique designs to benefit the community.

Example 5:
Methodical and highly enthusiastic Prince2 qualified project manager with over four years' progressive experience within the IT industry. Specialises in infrastructure-based projects and possesses a demonstrable track record of managing several award winning large-scale global projects worth £5m+.

Example 6:

Self-motivated, passionate soft skills trainer with fifteen years' experience in the design and presentation of training modules that have significantly boosted company productivity. Proven leadership, interpersonal and communication skills substantiated by motivating 4,000+ individuals towards academic and professional success.

Step 2: Career Objective

Should you be looking to change direction or draw upon experience from early on in your career, providing a career objective can help provide clarity and focus. Keep in succinct – just one sentence.

For example:

A candidate seeking to draw upon experience gained across the entire marketing mix and a performance record of increasing market share for underperformers in the market, may add to his or her profile that she is seeking to secure a role as a marketing strategist.

Step 3: Identify your USPs (unique selling points)

What makes you stand out from the competition? What have your delivered or achieved? In which areas have you added value or excelled? Begin sentences with a verb for example delivers, demonstrates, implements, achieves.

Example 1:

Talented, highly sought-after ACMA qualified financial controller with more than twenty years' experience working for two of the UK's most prominent investment banks. Proven ability to identify strategic and operational factors to drive profitability and enhance decision making.

- Implements systems and procedures to improve reporting, efficiencies or data accuracy, and increased shareholder value.
- Partners with senior stakeholders to drive strategic initiatives and transformation projects from design through to successful implementation, in an agile, 'can-do' style.

- Develops complex financial and forecasting models to optimise departmental and overall group performance including cash flow projections and funding requirements.

Example 2:
Seasoned senior manager with expertise encompassing web and mobile technology underpinned by ten years' progression with a leading telecommunications company.

- Project manages high-profile projects and effectively co-ordinates resource to achieve targets within stringent time constraints.
- Demonstrates in-depth analytical and strategic ability to facilitate operational and procedural planning.
- Committed towards ongoing personal development as demonstrated by the recent completion of an MBA at Brunel University.

When Writing Your Profile

1. **Keep it credible** – There is nothing that irks a reader more than big, powerful words and statements that cannot be validated in your CV. Provide evidence to back up your statements.
2. **Incorporate industry and technical terms relevant to your target position**.
3. **Don't provide a string of empty qualities** such as 'adaptable, hardworking, dedicated and enthusiastic individual who works well on own or as part of a team'. Or, 'relishes a challenge and is recognised as self-motivated, driven and ambitious'. These traits are better suited to a cover letter.
4. **Be factual** – Provide tangible examples that can be quantified wherever possible.
5. **Keep it concise** – don't waffle.
6. **Avoid sounding arrogant.**

Over the page are three tables. The first is a list of personal attributes; the second, a list of technical skills; and the third is a list of descriptive words. Whilst these lists are not exhaustive, they can be helpful when constructing your statement. Also refer to the Appendix at the end of the book for action words.

Table of personal attributes

Able	Dependable	Intelligent	Rational
Accomplished	Detail-oriented	Inventive	Realist
Adaptable	Determined	Loyal	Reliable
Adventurous	Diligent	Mature	Reputed
Alert	Diplomatic	Methodical	Resourceful
Ambitious	Dynamic	Meticulous	Responsible
Articulate	Effective	Motivated	Results-oriented
Assertive	Efficient	Multilingual	Self-assured
Astute	Empathetic	Observant	Self-confident
Award-winning	Energetic	Open-minded	Self-motivated
Bilingual	Enthusiastic	Organised	Self-reliant
Bright	Entrepreneurial	Outgoing	Sensitive
Calm	Established	Passionate	Spirited
Capable	Expert	Patient	Successful
Career-driven	Focused	People-oriented	Supportive
Caring	Friendly	Perceptive	Talented
Committed	Goal-driven	Persistent	Tenacious
Competent	Hands-on	Personable	Thorough
Confident	Hardworking	Positive attitude	Thoughtful
Conscientious	Helpful	Principled	Trustworthy
Consistent	High-energy	Proactive	Understanding
Co-operative	High-impact	Productive	Versatile
Creative	Honest	Professional	Willing
Cross-functional	Imaginative	Proficient	
Decisive	Independent	Qualified	
Dedicated	Innovative	Quick-thinking	

Table of technical skills

Account management	Business process re-	Crisis resolution
Administration	engineering	CRM strategies
Analytical	Business transformation	Customer service
Business analysis	Change management	Data validation
Business development	Cost reduction	Decision making

Delegation	Negotiation	development
Design	Networking	Resource management
Due diligence	Operations	Sales management
Financial accounting	management	Stakeholder
Financial analysis	Organisational planning	management
Financial planning	Planning	Start ups
Financial reporting	Problem solving	Strategic management
KPI development	Process improvement	Strategic planning
Leadership	Product development	Technical analysis
Management	Programme	Time management
accounting	management	Training and
Marketing mix	Project management	development
Marketing strategy	Re-branding	
Mergers & acquisitions	Research and	

Table of descriptive words

Able	Displays	Natural	Skilled
Accomplished	Engenders	Outstanding	Solid
Accustomed to	Equipped	Participated	Strong
Acquired	Established	Possesses	Superb
Adept	Exceptional	Practised	Superior
Awarded	Exhibits	Profit-driving	Talented
Boasts	Extensive	Recognised	Track record
Broad	Focused	Refined	Trained
Capable	Gained	Regarded	Well-defined
Delivers	Honed	Renowned	Well-respected
Demonstrated	In-depth	Reputed	Wide-ranging
Developed	Instils	Seasoned	

Tip

Tailor your profile to the job being applied for. Determine what skills, experience and background the employer is after and use the same terminology.

CHAPTER 8

Key Skills

For those with over two years of experience you would look to create a dedicated 'Key Skills' section immediately below your profile statement. For more junior CVs, key skills can be presented separately but it is more common to incorporate them into your profile statement and/or cover letter.

This chapter will help you identify and compile core and/or transferable skills most relevant to your target position.

'A skill is defined as, 'the ability, coming from one's knowledge, practice, aptitude etc., to perform an activity very well.'

'A transferable skill is defined as, 'skills and knowledge gained throughout your life whether it be during employment, sport, parenting, hobbies etc., that are then applicable and transferable to what you do in your next job.'

Benefits of a Key Skills Section

A dedicated 'Key Skills' section is a great opportunity to showcase relevant or transferable skills. As organisations are increasingly using ATS (Applicant Tracking System) software to pre-screen CVs, incorporating keywords is vital to your CV being found and ultimately shortlisted.

'I really like a skills section on a CV – use a few relevant headings and then list the related skills below. It's an easy way to bring your skills together and makes what you have to offer easily scannable, rather than having to read all through your CV to find them.'

DANIELL MORRISEY, SENIOR EDITORIAL EARLY CAREERS SCHEMES MANAGER AT THE BBC

Identifying Key Skills

It is important to distinguish between soft and hard skills:

Soft Skills:

The Collins English Dictionary defines 'soft skills' as 'desirable qualities for certain forms of employment that do not depend on acquired knowledge: they include common sense, the ability to deal with people and a positive flexible attitude.'

Below is a list of 'soft skills' but the list is not exhaustive and should be used as a guideline only.

Accountability	Integrity	Problem-solving
Adaptability	Interpersonal	Professionalism
Communication	Lateral thinking	Public speaking
Creativity	Leadership	Punctual
Courteous	Listening	Responsible
Crisis resolution	Logical thinking	Self-confidence
Decision-making	Mentoring	Self-motivation
Delegating	Motivating	Teamwork
Dependability	Multi-tasking	Technical literacy
Emotional awareness	Negotiating	Time management
Flexibility	Networking	Troubleshooter
Initiative	Organisation	Work ethic
Innovation	Positive attitude	Writing

Hard Skills:

Hard skills include technical or administrative competence. Refer to page 46–7 for a reminder of technical skills.

Entry-level jobseekers:
Consider skills gained during studies, an internship, a work placement, voluntary or part-time work. Given your limited experience, the focus will more likely be on soft skills.

Those with more established careers:
Consider skills relevant to your target position with more emphasis on technical skills. Soft skills can be emphasised in your cover letter.

Should you be looking to apply for roles where you have little or no experience, identify your transferable skills,i.e qualities that can be transferred from one job to another. Prominence would be on soft skills..

Below are ways to establish which skills you should be highlighting:

1. **If you are responding to a specific position:** Gather information from the job advertisement, job description, and/or person specification to establish what skills they specify as 'must have' and 'nice to have'.

   If the skills required are radically different to your own, rethink whether the job is a viable opportunity.

2. **If you are applying speculatively:** Research the company to determine what skills and attributes they look for in an employee. Read through job advertisements of similar roles to establish what skills they typically require.

Tip

Incorporate additional skills that may support your application. Speak with colleagues, peers and friends to reveal skills you may take for granted. Old performance appraisals can also be enlightening.

Compiling your Key Skills Section
This section can be entitled 'Key Skills' or 'Key Strengths' in more junior CVs, or 'Keywords', 'Major Competencies', 'Key Skills' or 'Areas of Expertise' in more senior level CVs.

How much detail, if any, you provide under each skill will depend on the CV type you have selected. Each CV type will be discussed separately.

1. Chronological CVs

For candidates with more than two years of experience, identify between ten and twelve core skills that best describe your abilities and are most appropriate to your target position. These can be listed in columns on your CV.

For those with less experience, keywords could be in a separate section or spread across your profile, work history and cover letter.

Example 1: Business Analyst

- Business analysis
- Project management
- Quality control
- Agile methodologies
- Scrum methodologies
- User stories
- Flow diagrams
- Product development lifecycle
- Complex data analysis
- Team leadership

Example 2: Call Centre Manager/Team Leader

- Customer service
- Organisation and planning
- Interpersonal and communication
- Conflict resolution
- Team management
- Full project life-cycle management
- Process improvement
- Stakeholder management
- Call handling

Example 3: Change Manager

- Change management
- Crisis management
- Product development
- Strategic planning
- Process improvement
- Lean six sigma
- Team leadership
- Stakeholder management
- Project management
- Complex financial analysis

- Programme management
- Relationship management
- Business transformation
- Operational best practices

Example 4: Graduate

- Leadership
- Team player
- Administration
- Customer focus
- Research
- Organisation and prioritisation

Example 5: Accountant

- Strategic planning
- Transformational change
- KPI development
- Financial reporting
- Financial planning & analysis
- Financial modelling
- Advanced excel
- Process improvement
- Mergers and acquisitions
- Due diligence
- Cash flow management

Example 6: Sales & Marketing Professional

- Marketing Solutions
- Project management
- Re-branding
- Research
- Product development
- Account management
- Relationship management
- Business development
- Stakeholder management
- Networking
- Team leadership
- Presentation skills
- Exhibitions & shows
- Client briefings
- Referral business

Example 7: Business Consultant

- Service management
- Project management
- Programme management
- Start-ups
- Training and development
- Business development
- Marketing solutions
- Brand development
- Business process improvement
- Strategic design

2. Hybrid CVs

If you have opted for a hybrid CV, choose up to six skills and list them in order of importance. Under each skill, provide up to three examples of where you demonstrated this skill with the focus on achievements.

Example 1: Team Leader – Call Centre

Organisation
- Prioritises, schedules and co-ordinates workload as demonstrated whilst ...
- Effectively organises team workloads, utilising the personal strengths of individuals to maximise results.

People Management
- Seasoned manager with experience of managing and mentoring large multi-cultural teams of up to 20 people. Improved attrition rate of staff following the introduction of an incentive scheme.
- Significantly enhanced customer satisfaction levels; improved declining retention levels by 20% within just twelve months.

Presenting
- Accomplished presenter having prepared and conducted several high-pressure presentations to audiences of up to 30 people.
- Gained good presentation skills through project work at university and through former role as a ...

Problem Solving
- Logical and lateral thinker able to act quickly and efficiently to resolve complex problems.
- Commended by colleagues for utilising initiative to resolve complex problems, including ...

Relationship Management
- Increased company revenue by 12% in one year; forged strong

53

relationships with customers which generated extensive repeat business.

Example 2: Junior Accountant

Financial Analysis

- Completed several research projects during studies, which involved the detailed analysis of company financials, share price and dividend policy.
- Accustomed to using financial models such as ... and ...
- Gained a good understanding of accounting principles through studies and relevant work experience.

Project Management

- Successfully demonstrated project skills by <provide an example>.
- Demonstrable record of delivering high quality projects on time and to budget including successful delivery of ...

Report Writing

- Experience of preparing several essays and papers in a methodical and organised manner during degree course.
- Highly developed report writing skills for both technical and non-technical audiences.

Customer Service

- Consistently commended by customers for being supportive, helpful and for exceeding their expectations.
- Acquired two major clients which contributed 5% to bottom-line profitability.

Example 3: PA

Administration

- Commended by management for being highly organised with good planning and time management skills.

- Adept at maintaining accurate records as demonstrated as a data entry clerk; achieved 99.5% accuracy, well beyond colleagues.

Communication
- Possesses excellent communication skills, written and verbal, and is equipped to communicate effectively at all levels.
- Through various part-time roles, honed the ability to engage and build rapport with a wide range of people.

Computer/Technical skills
- Highly computer literate with a strong technical understanding of various programmes and systems including Microsoft Office and Sage.
- Impressive keyboard skills at 80 wpm, coupled with a high level of accuracy.

Customer Service
- Consistently commended by customers for being supportive, helpful and for exceeding their expectations.

Example 4: Customer Service Executive
Customer Focus
- Identifies customer requirements and provides solutions to meet their individual needs.
- Maintains regular communication with key accounts and supports the sales process, deputising in the absence of the sales manager.

Communication
- Cultivated a talent for communicating effectively with people from diverse cultures and backgrounds through working at a variety of multi-nationals.

- Practised at effectively dealing with and resolving complaints from difficult, demanding customers.

Relationship Building
- Adept at engaging with and forging long-standing relationships with customers and colleagues alike.
- Engenders trust with customers by displaying absolute integrity in all business transactions.

Example 5: Sales Manager
Business Development/Sales
- Increased the visibility and profile of company XYZ though attending monthly networking events and seminars.
- Boosted bottom-line profitability by 22% in nine-month period; defined target market, formulated effective marketing strategies and identified new business opportunities.

Training
- In collaboration with senior management, identified training needs and development plans for all sales personnel across the whole of the UK.
- Developed the content for a training manual at X YZ company that is still being utilised today.
- Delivers one-to-one coaching and training sessions, on both technical and customer service requirements, to all areas of the business.

Communicating/Presenting
- Exhibits strong communication skills, both written and verbal, and is adept with communicating effectively with people at all levels.
- An accomplished presenter who is able to present information clearly and is skilled with engaging an audience.

- Liaises daily with suppliers and customers to ensure the smooth delivery of goods and services.

3. Skills-based/Functional CVs

The skills section will form the focus of your CV. Identify up to six transferrable skills and list them in order of importance.

Under each skill, provide two to three demonstrable examples/achievements; these can relate to any aspect of your life, whether it be a skill gained through a sporting interest, a project managed or voluntary work. Keep examples relevant and ideally current, i.e. within the last five years. It is, however, acceptable to draw upon early experience.

Example 1:

A person seeking a role in Customer Service may look to highlight Communication, Relationship Building, Customer Focus and perhaps Administration skills.

Customer Focus

- A good listener who is skilled at identifying customer requirements and providing solutions to meet their individual needs.
- Maintains regular communication with key accounts and supports the sales process, deputising in the absence of the sales manager.

Communication

- Cultivated a talent to communicate effectively with people from diverse cultures and backgrounds through working at a variety of multi-nationals.
- Practised at effectively dealing with and resolving complaints from difficult, demanding customers.

Relationship Building

- Adept at engaging with and forging long-standing relationships with customers and colleagues alike.

- Engenders trust with customers by displaying absolute integrity in all business transactions.

Administration

- Managed the stationary requirements and equipment maintenance for a busy office of up to 40 staff.
- Designed and implemented a new system that improved the accuracy of client records.
- In-depth experience of minute taking, diary management and handling correspondence.

Example 2:

An individual with diverse experience seeking to secure a position in sales may wish to emphasise very similar skills to the above but may include 'Business Development/Sales', and also change the order in which the skills are presented.

Business Development/Sales

- As a telemarketer, acquired 20 new accounts within the first month of joining and was acknowledged as 'Employee of the Month'.
- Increased the visibility and profile of company XYZ though attending monthly networking events and seminars.
- Increased bottom-line profitability by 22% in a nine-month period; redefined the target market, formulated effective marketing strategies and identified new business opportunities.

Customer Focus

- Maintains regular communication with key accounts and supports the sales process, deputising in the absence of the sales manager.
- A good listener who is skilled at identifying customer requirements and providing solutions to meet their individual needs.

Communication
- Practised at effectively dealing with and resolving complaints from difficult, demanding customers.
- Cultivated a talent to communicate effectively with people from diverse cultures and backgrounds through working at a variety of multi-nationals.

Relationship Building
- Increased revenue received from existing customer base by 15% in first six months. Nurtured relationships and engendered trust with customers by displaying absolute integrity in all business transactions.

Example 3:
In this example, the individual is looking to draw upon vast experience gained in a variety of roles across a number of industries to secure a training role in the public sector.

Training
- Prepared and delivered several in-house training programmes to hotel staff.
- In collaboration with senior management, identified training needs and development plans for their individual teams.
- Developed the content for a training manual at XYZ company that is still being utilised today.
- Experience of delivering one-to-one coaching and training sessions, on both technical and customer service requirements, to all areas of the business.

Communication/Presentation
- Exhibits strong communication skills, both written and verbal, and is adept at communicating effectively with people at all levels.

- An accomplished presenter who is able to present information clearly and is skilled with engaging an audience.
- Liaises daily with suppliers and customers to ensure the smooth delivery of goods and services.

Organisation/Planning
- Manages accurate staff records for 300+ employees; prioritises and schedules tasks effectively, delegating responsibility where necessary.
- Managed an office relocation project; effectively moved and rehoused 200 staff and all office equipment within three days with limited business interruption.
- Successfully co-ordinated and planned several corporate events for up to 500 people, including all catering and entertainment.

Relationship Management
- Skilled with developing and maintaining good working relationships with internal and external customers.
- Forges strong relationships with key players in the industry, developing mutually beneficial relationships that result in objectives being surpassed.

Management
- A natural leader with experience of managing and motivating teams of up to 10 staff.
- Reputed for providing direction to and developing multi-cultural teams.

Computer Literacy
- Fully conversant with Microsoft Office, including PowerPoint, Word and Publisher.
- Good understanding of various design packages including Photoshop.

Tip

One of the best ways to ensure your CV is ATS optimised is to pack your CV with appropriate keywords, meaning those specified in job descriptions of your target position. This will maximise your chances of being short-listed.

CHAPTER 9

Educational Background

The next step in the process is to detail your education, qualifications, professional development and training.

The amount of detail that needs to be provided and where the information is presented will depend on how much work experience you have.

Candidates with Less Than Two Years' Experience

As an entry-level job seeker, your educational history is going to be of most interest to a prospective employer and hence, it must form the focus of your CV. It will be presented immediately after your 'profile statement' or 'key skills' section.

Detailing your education

Select an appropriate heading: 'Education', 'Education and Qualifications', 'Education and Training' or 'Educational History'. The information should be listed in reverse chronological order, i.e. most recent first.

1. Degrees

Provide degree name, institution, to what level (honours), classification and start/end dates. Include any dissertations or final year projects, followed by core subjects/modules and grade. Where top grades have been achieved in a particular subject, insert the details. Degrees should be abbreviated, for example, Bachelor of Science should be written as BSc.

TIP

The correct way to spell bachelor's degree is with the apostrophe. The 's' in bachelor's indicates a possessive (the degree of a bachelor), not a plural. If referring to a specific degree, capitalise bachelor and avoid creating a possessive: Bachelor of Commerce. The same rules apply to a master's degree.

Example 1:

BSc in Economics, York University: 2:1   20XX-20XX

Dissertation: 'An analysis of ...'

Core Modules: Microeconomics, Macroeconomics, Econometrics and Quantitative Techniques

Example 2:

Queen Mary, University of London:

20XX–Date   **MSc in Chemical Process Engineering**
                              Core Modules: Process Dynamic & Control, Fluid Particle Systems, Safety & Loss Prevention

20XX-20XX   **BSc (Hons) in Chemical Engineering: 2:1**
                              Core Modules: Process Dynamics, Environmental Engineering, Heat Transfer Operation

2. Diplomas and college education

Provide diploma name, institution, dates, grade achieved, i.e. pass, merit, credit or level achieved, and the modules or subjects completed. Where top grades have been achieved in a particular subject, insert the details. Diplomas should be abbreviated, for example BTEC National Diploma.

Example 1:

HND, West London University: 72%   20XX-20XX

Example 2:

ABC College of Further Education:

BTEC National Diploma in Engineering – Merit	**20XX-20XX**
BTEC First Diploma in Engineering – Merit	**20XX-20XX**
NVC, Engineering Assembly Level 1	**20XX-20XX**

3. Courses and certifications

Provide the course name or certification, institution and the year awarded.

Example 1:

NCFE Certificate, Computer Technology, 20XX

City & Guilds Certificate, Computer Aided Design, 20XX

Example 2:

20XX	Community Sports Leadership Award (CSLA)
20XX	First Aid Course

4. School education

Provide details of the number of 'A' levels, 'AS' Levels, GCSEs or Scottish Highers attained. Summarise your GCSEs, providing only top grades.

Example 1:

3 'A' Levels, St Mary's School for Girls   20XX-20XX

Subjects: English (A), Mathematics (B), Business Studies (B)

8 GCSEs grades A–C/6–9 including Mathematics (7) and English (8) 20XX-20XX

Example 2:

4 'A' Levels, X YZ College, Southampton   20XX-20XX

Physics (B), Economics (B), General Studies (C), Biology (B)

9 GCSEs, X YZ School, Romsey   20XX-20XX

Grades A–B/7–9 including Mathematics (8), English (7) and Science(9)

5.Achievements/Highlights and Leadership Roles.

This section can be separate (directly below education) or incorporated under Education.

5.1 Achievements

Showcase achievements during studies. Include commendations, awards, competitions won, initiatives introduced, academic achievements and scholarships. Sporting triumphs can be included here or under additional information at the end of your CV.

Examples
- Awarded Academic Excellence Award in Year 10
- Published an article in the Daily Express entitled '...'
- Participated in an Exchange Programme at XYZ University
- Achieved top of class for two consecutive years in both Maths and Science
- Received a special award from the Head of English in recognition of...
- Achieved distinctions in Corporate Finance and Control Systems in final year of master's degree.

5.2 Leadership roles

Furnish examples of leadership roles undertaken at school, college, or university. These can include appointment as a prefect, student representative or team captain through to leading group discussions or founding societies.

Examples
- Elected representative for the student body.
- Appointed as Head Prefect.
- Co-founded the Chinese society; organised several social events and provided help to students experiencing social problems.

- Appointed president of the diver's club for two consecutive years.
- Led group discussions for final year project.
- Won two regional awards as Director of the Young Enterprise Group.
- Attained the History Prize for the highest grade in school.
- Received Bronze Duke of Edinburgh award.

Tip

Academics may find it necessary to include an Appendix, i.e. a separate page detailing qualifications and professional development.

Candidates with More Than Two Years' Experience

At this level, your career history is going to be of more interest to a prospective employer. Consequently, this section need not be very detailed and would appear after your work experience.

Refer to points one to four above for heading and how to present education. Detail of subjects, grades and dissertations are not required unless you achieved a first degree, straight As or something extraordinary.

Courses, certifications received or seminars attended can be included below qualifications. If the list is exhaustive, include only those relevant to your target role.

Detailing your education

Select an appropriate heading: 'Education', 'Education and Qualifications', 'Education and Professional Development', 'Education and Training', or 'Education and Certifications'.

It is here that you would highlight your education and qualifications, and list any special courses passed, certifications received or seminars attended.

Your educational history should be listed in reverse chronological order, i.e. most recent first. Provide the name of the qualification, the institution, the dates you completed or expect to complete your studies.

Example 1:

MBA, Heriot-Watt University, Edinburgh   2001

BSc (Hons) Elec Eng with Computer Science, UCT   1992

Certificate in Quantitative Finance, 7city, London   Ongoing

Mathematics for Quantitative Finance, 7city, London   2006

Example 2:

BA (Hons) Degree in Business Studies, Warwick University, 1995

HND in Business & Finance, Kingston College, 1993

Example 3:

Various in-house courses including:

Basic Food Hygiene & Employee Relationship Course   2005

First Aid Certificate   2003

Two 'O' Levels   2002

Example 4:

1998 BTEC Foundation course in Art and Design

1996 Two 'A' Levels in Art and General Studies

1994 Six GCSEs including Mathematics and English

Example 5:

BENG (Hons) in Telecommunications, University of Essex   2005

Certifications:

MSTC Microsoft Windows Mobile 5.0: Configuration   2003

MCSE Windows Server   2003

Courses:

Leadership Programme, in-house

Presentation Skills, in-house

Pointers

- Include only the date you completed the qualification.
- If you have a degree, it is not necessary to provide details of schooling.
- If your education was a long time ago, dates can be omitted.
- Separate professional qualifications from courses, and list them from highest level of attainment to lowest.

Obstacles You May Face

- **Poor grades**

It is important not to include or draw attention to anything negative on a CV, and as such, it is recommended that any grades below average be omitted.

For those with over two years' experience, grades need not be provided.

- **No real education to speak of**

Employers are interested in your highest level of attainment and as such include this section even if GCSE is the highest level. Include any courses attended.

- **Incomplete qualification**

Perhaps you embarked on further education but never completed it; omit the qualification if it doesn't create an obvious gap. Why draw attention to something if avoidable? Otherwise, place in brackets (incomplete) and include the details of subjects passed if relevant.

- **Your qualification is ongoing**

If you are still studying, simply state as 'ongoing', or express as 20XX– Date, or state expected completion date.

- **Education completed abroad**

Job seekers from abroad are habitually looking to work and practise in the area for which they have been trained. As such, it may be necessary to convert your qualifications to the UK equivalent. This can be achieved by contacting one of the following national agencies below. This is particularly important if you require a certain qualification or grade in order to apply for the role.

UK Naric – Official provider of information on international qualifications for over 180 countries (www.naric.org.uk).

UK NRP – Evaluate international vocational qualifications (www.uknrp.org. uk).

• **Poor command of the English language**

Where English is not your first language, consider completing the IELTS or the TOEIC tests to enhance marketability.

1. The IELTS (International English Language Testing System)

This testing system assesses language abilities and tests listening, reading, writing and speaking capabilities.

IELTS is jointly managed by:
• University of Cambridge ESOL Examinations;
• British Council;
• IDP Education Australia: IELTS Australia.

There are many practise exams that can be completed online and many test centres across the UK, most of which are colleges and universities.

The global website is: www.ielts.org.

2. TOEIC (Test of English for International Communication)

This test is designed to evaluate the listening and reading skills of non-native speakers who need to use English in the workplace. It is administered as open public sessions, and at companies and language schools around the world.

TOEIC was developed and is administered by ETS, a US-based, non-profit institution. The test is widely accepted by corporations, English language programs, and government agencies around the world.

As with IELTS, you can undertake online preparation courses. Tests take place at various language centres across the UK.

Tip

If it is a prerequisite of a job opportunity to have a particular qualification, make reference to it in your profile statement or present education on page one of your CV.

CHAPTER 10

Work History

This section focuses on your work experience. It is here you will provide detail of which companies you have worked for and when, job titles, responsibilities and, most importantly, your achievements.

The key is to focus on achievements. Prospective employers, hiring authorities and recruitment agents do not want to read a list of duties and responsibilities. They know what an accountant or sales manager does on a day-to-day basis. What they want to know is what you have achieved for each of the companies you have worked for.

An achievement is defined as, 'something accomplished successfully, especially by means of exertion, skill, practice or perseverance'.

An achievement is unique to your experience and is your opportunity to provide evidence of your abilities. Demonstrating what you have achieved in the past provides a prospective employer with a good insight into what you can achieve in the future. Past performance is a predictor of future performance.

As such, this area will receive a lot of attention from a prospective employer. This chapter covers how to write effective, interesting content. It includes expert opinions, examples and help with overcoming common problems.

Chronological and Hybrid/Combined CVs

This next section is split into candidates with less than and candidates with more than two years' work experience, as what you emphasise will be dependent on how much experience you have.

Candidates with less than two years' work experience

First-time job seekers are often unsure of what and how much to include. Many discount summer jobs or voluntary work; all experience is relevant.

'A common thing with university level graduates, they assume that the summer job they had, that was essentially to earn pocket money, is not relevant. To us it's very relevant if somebody has had the get-up-and-go to work 20 hours a week to supplement their pocket money, and help them fund their way through college.'

JONATHAN JONES, HEAD OF TALENT AT ROIVANT PHARMA

'Your experience could be in sports where you've organised a competition or at school where you've organised a trip. I'm looking for the skills that are relevant to the role.'

MARK THOMAS, TALENT ACQUISITION AND DEVELOPMENT DIRECTOR AT ABCAM

Whether you have worked as a cashier, a dog walker or a sales assistant, you are bound to have gained or honed some very valuable skills. Holding down a summer or a part-time job also tells a prospective employer a lot about you. So, include it all – everything from summer jobs and internships through to voluntary work experience, no matter how trivial the role may seem.

Compiling the content

This section can be headed 'Work Experience', 'Work History' or 'Employment History'. If you have had or are currently in a full-time role, you could split your work history into 'Work Experience' and 'Professional Experience'. 'Work Experience' is often considered to be summer or part-time work or could include internships. Any voluntary work should be expressed separately and is covered in a separate chapter.

Begin by writing down all your positions, starting with the most recent and working backwards. Detail the company name, location, start/end dates, and your job title. Leave half a page between each role providing you with space to add a number of bullet points under each role. It is often valuable to provide a short description of the company below the company name, particularly if the company is obscure.

The type of information you can include under each of your roles are:

1. Duties and responsibilities
Describe what you were brought on to do (denote main tasks and responsibilities) and how the opportunity arose. This should be summarised in one-two sentences at most.

Example 1 – Part-time waitress:
- Recruited to serve up to 30 customers a night over two covers at this exclusive, high-end fish restaurant. Provides consistently high levels of customer service and works closely with Front of House and Head Chef to deliver a memorable dining experience.

2. Initiatives introduced
Consider including proposals or ideas you recommended to improve processes or procedures.

Examples:
- Developed an Excel spreadsheet that considerably enhanced the accuracy of information and eliminated duplication of data.
- Designed a rating system that accessed the quality of potential leads and significantly improved revenue potential.
- Created an insightful proposal for a knowledge-sharing platform to improve visibility of information across the business; it was presented to and accepted by senior management.

3. Examples of money made or saved for the company
Companies are in business to make money so if you can provide examples at this early stage in your career as to how you may have made

or saved money for a company, this will be of great interest to a prospective employer.

Examples:

- In conjunction with the Sales Director, secured a deal with a major retailer, worth £100k per annum.
- Introduced and implemented a process that improved web conversions by 250%.

4. Targets met and exceeded – company and personal

As with the point above, the ability to meet or exceed company targets demonstrates your ability to make money and shows drive. The ability to meet your own personal targets displays focus and commitment.

Example:

- Consistently met and exceeded sales targets and was rewarded with a 'Top Account Opener' award and £500 within first two months of joining.

5. Promotions or offers of full-time employment

Receiving an advancement or being offered a permanent position demonstrates your potential to a prospective employer, particularly if it occurs within a short timescale.

Example:

- Promoted to Supervisor of XYZ Company after a period of four months, becoming the youngest supervisor within XYZ Franchise.

6. Emphasise team working and/or leadership capabilities

Provide details of any projects you may have worked on or managed. Include examples of where you were involved in training or supporting staff, and anything else that will demonstrate your ability to lead or work as part of a team.

Examples:
- Worked as part of a team to plan, design and deliver an intranet for a PR company.
- Managed a small team of four Administrators across two branches and provided product training to all new starters.

7. Honing or learning new skills

Specify any skills and knowledge gained or learned particularly if those skills will be relevant to your target position. These can include anything from honing problem-solving skills and resolving customer queries through to leadership and communication skills.

Examples:
- Gained an excellent knowledge of the principles of book-keeping and accountancy.
- Developed event management skills from assisting with the co-ordination of various high profile events.

8. Awards

Have you received any awards in recognition for a job well done?

Example:
- Awarded 'Employee of the Month' for consistently exceeding customer expectations.

9. Commendations

Have you received praise, written or verbal, from a colleague, manager, peer or client? Including one or two recommendations can validate your worth to a company.

Example:
- Commended by the Team Leader for providing consistently high levels of customer service and for remaining calm in heated situations.

10. Other accomplishments

Include anything else that you have been particularly proud of.

How to express the information

1. Detail the company name, location, job title and whether part- or full-time, or an internship. Include start and end dates.
2. Provide a description of the company in one sentence. If space is an issue, this can be incorporated into the next section.
3. In a couple of sentences, define what you were brought on to do – the scope of the role, your duties and responsibilities.
4. Using bullet points, describe what you have achieved using points 2 through 9 above. First, define the achievement, outcome or result, furnish tangible examples and quantify wherever possible. Then express how this was achieved or what your personal involvement was. Use the action words at the end of the book to help you with this section.

Pointers

- Aim to provide up to three points under each role. If a short summer job, it is fine to have just one point.
- If you have too many points, include those statements that are most impressive.
- Avoid stating the obvious and listing a job description.
- If involved in a detailed project, begin with the outcome and then provide a couple of bullets below to describe your personal involvement.
- Do not include anything negative.
- Include what you have done, not things that you still hope to do.
- Place your most impressive statements first.

Potential Problems

1. Obscure job title

Should you have held obscure or company specific job titles, generalise the title so you appeal to the widest possible audience.

2. Many positions held

Ideally, include all your work experience but if you have held more than four/five roles, only include detail on those roles:

- most appropriate to your target position; or
- where you made an impact; or
- where you gained/honed key skills that will be relevant to a prospective employer.

The balance of your experience can be summarised with merely the company name, job title and start/end dates. Or it can be omitted if no obvious gap is created.

3. No work experience

Should you have no work experience, voluntary or otherwise, emphasise other areas in your CV, for example, key skills gained during your studies. Also provide information on any other activities that you may or have been involved in whether it be sporting interests or hobbies.

Examples

Below are some examples of what content to include under work history and some different ways in which the information can be presented.

Example 1:

ABC Pub Ltd, London **Jan 2019–Sept 2019**

Recruited on a part-time basis to serve clients food and beverages in this sports bar.

Bartender (Part-time)

- Developed customer facing skills and the ability to remain calm and professional within a fast-paced working environment.
- Successfuly co-ordinated and hosted private and public functions for up to 50 people, honing organisational and planning skills.

- Assisted with training new staff members.
- Reduced shrinkage; monitored and maintained stock levels.

Example 2:

Summer 2016   **Cashier, XYZ Limited, Hampshire**

- Performed general cashier duties for VIP customers, honing customer service and cash handling capabilities.
- Consistently cross-sold company products and services to new and existing clients; received an 'employee of the month' award for two consecutive months for highest product sales.

Example 3:

Sept 2016–Dec 2016   **ABC plc**

Assistant Event Manager

Recruited on short-term contract to assist this event management company over its busy period, providing full secretarial and administrative support to a team of three event managers.

- Organised a variety of high-profile events and functions including themed evenings and fund raising events for up to 200 people, all of which were highly successful and achieved high attendance rates.
- Gained time management skills and honed the ability to work well under pressure.

Example 4:

Sept 2017 to Date: Administrator, XTC Limited, London

Appointed to handle all office administration for this busy firm of accountants, consisting of fifteen employees and a client base of 2,000.

- Increased productivity levels and reduced duplication of effort; created and maintained an access database to accurately log all incoming client calls.
- Reduced the amount of time required to locate and access client files; re-organised the entire company filing system, a three-month project.

- Successfully cleared all outstanding filing and a backlog of data entry tasks during this period.

May 2016 to Sept 2016: PA, RLC Limited, London
Recruited to manage the Sales Director's daily schedule and deal with all incoming and outgoing mail.

- Built strong relationships with foreign clients; maintained daily contact with clients, updating them of any contract changes.
- Gained valuable communication skills and the ability to effectively manage a heavy workload under pressure.

Example 5:
ABC plc, London   **Jan 2018–Sept 2020**
Medical Technologist (Internship)
Recruited to shadow the Head of Microbiology; helped prepare and analyse the results of blood and bodily fluids.

- Received detailed training within Microbiology and Cytology departments.
- Investigated and analysed clinical specimens, reporting results to the relevant medical staff.

Example 6:
May 2017 to Date: Law Clerk, DGH Limited, London
Hired to provide administrative support to lawyers; conducted research and drafted court documents.

- Booked various appointments for associates and senior partners.
- Proof read legal documents for various senior partners.
- Participated in two mock trials, developing communication skills and confidence.

Sept 2015 to Dec 2016: Sales Agent, SRC plc, Surrey
Appointed part-time to promote products and services of this large supplier of office stationery. Reported directly to the Head of Sales and supported a team of four Sales Managers.

- Initiated business launches for potential customers to demonstrate product range.
- Devised a new sales pitch and approach, which was later adopted by the entire team.
- Consistently converted new enquiries into sales; received several financial rewards in recognition.
- Gained persuasion and negotiation skills.

Candidates With More Than Two Years' Work Experience

A common pitfall is that people tend to produce a job description rather than focusing on what they have achieved or what skills or knowledge they have gained or honed. We all know that it is an accountant's job to produce a set of year-end accounts or that it is a sales professional's role to bring on new business. Do not risk patronising or alienating the reader by stating the obvious. Instead, explain what you have delivered in relation to your duties and responsibilities, providing tangible examples and quantifying wherever possible.

'The biggest thing that I look for in a CV is legacy; so, what value has an individual added to their particular organisation during the time in which they've done a particular role? So, what I'm particularly looking at is contribution to bottom line profitability and sales. What are the metrics, what are the key performance indicators that that person has been responsible for and what have they personally delivered.'
MARK THOMAS, TALENT ACQUISITION AND DEVELOPMENT DIRECTOR AT ABCAM

'What we're really looking for is evidence of what somebody's done in their lives, not evidence of what they think they are.'
WILL DAWKINS, PARTNER AT SPENCER STEWART

As a way of reflecting how your accomplishments will sell your ability to an employer, a CV should have a good combination of features and benefits. Adrian Cojocaru uses the analogy of someone looking to purchase a car.

'If you go and buy a car, you know that the features of the car are: alloy wheels, a big stereo and a big engine. The benefits are: low fuel consumption, low CO2 emissions, it was voted the best car for three consecutive years and families with kids prefer it. So again, you want to know the features of the person but you also want to know the benefits. The benefits would need to be very precise and descriptive, detailing what a person has achieved.'

ADRIAN COJOCARU, DIRECTOR AT TABERNAM SKINNER LTD

Compiling the Content

This section can be headed 'Work History', 'Professional Experience', 'Employment History' or 'Career History'.

Note down all of your roles since leaving school, college or university starting with the most recent and working backwards. Detail the company name, location, start/end dates and your job title. Employers, hiring authorities or recruitment agents are only interested in the last ten years, so any roles beyond that can be summarised, unless particularly relevant to your target position. The idea is to provide a lot of detail for roles undertaken in the last five years and less so thereafter.

Begin by providing detail under your most recent role and work backwards:

1. Company name

Provide a brief description of the company, particularly if the company is not a household name. Include the size and scope of the business such as the number of employees, turnover and its reputation/financial standing.

2. Job title

Keep this relatively generic so it appeals to the widest audience and is recognised by the ATS.

3. Duties and responsibilities

In no more than two or three sentences, provide an overview of what you were recruited to do. Include how the role came about; the scope of the role; where you fit into the reporting structure; whether you are involved in training, coaching, KPIs or target setting; and, where applicable, team size, budget and P&L responsibility.

Example: Administrator

- Recruited to maintain and develop the department's filing system and deal with ad hoc requests from four senior managers.
- Provide customer support, handling queries received via email and on the phone.

4. Achievements

Reflect on your achievements and accomplishments in line with what you were brought on to do. Focus on your personal involvement, the impact/outcomes of your actions and the business benefit. It is often difficult for people to think about successes they have had or the impact they have made. Below are some triggers which should help you identify what you have achieved. Consider examples of where you:

4.1 Introduced an initiative

Consider any proposals or ideas you recommended, designed or implemented that saved time, money or improved processes. This can be as simple as developing an Excel spreadsheet to improve the accuracy of information, through to implementing a new process or system that reduced operational costs.

Example:

- Reduced double handling of equipment and increased quality of the end product; redesigned layout of the warehouse facility which was later rolled out nationally.

4.2 Made or saved money, time or resource

Companies are in business to make money so it is important, where possible, to provide examples of where you have made or saved money, time or resource.

Examples:

- Improved reliability of company payroll and saved £40k per year; received approval to outsource the company's payroll.
- Played instrumental role in increasing company revenue by 30% per annum; secured two new clients for XYZ Company.
- Instigated a project saving plan across several product areas of the group; gained Board approval to implement the company's first-ever procurement solution worth £2m.
- Streamlined procedures in the finance department resulting in an immediate cost saving of £0.5m. Saved a further £0.25m per annum by sourcing new suppliers and securing above average discounts.
- Saved the company £10m over a three-year period, four times more than anticipated; delivered a high standard of operation and budgetary control to XYZ County Council.
- Turned around a previously declining portfolio to an impressive 125% year-on-year revenue growth within eight months of being appointed by ...
- Substantially reduced production costs by 15% whilst maintaining quality; designed and developed specialised moulding products that ...
- Reduced operational costs by 7% per annum following a series of negotiations with current suppliers.
- Delivered 40% revenue growth in two years; orchestrated the successful turnaround of ABC business unit by revitalising the product range and sales strategy.

4.3 Met or exceeded company targets or expectations

The ability to meet or exceed targets or expectations will demonstrate drive and commitment. Provide examples of where or how this has been achieved and the overall benefit to company, client or supplier.

Example:

- Acquired three new accounts over a six week period with estimated revenue of £95k per annum; built client trust via introduction of a consultative selling approach which helped secure a client who had been on the company's radar for several years.
- Consistently exceed quarterly sales targets of £75k, achieving 20% higher than any other colleague.
- Achieved highest ever-average occupancy rate for a hotel in the Bahamas (92%) in 2019 and doubled room revenue over the same period.
- Secured customer satisfaction levels of 4 Star or higher throughout 2018 as recorded on Trust Pilot; provided consistently high levels of customer service and trained junior team members to do the same.
- Awarded 'Regional Sales Person of the Year' for three consecutive years; consistently exceeded set targets and outperformed peers as forged long-standing relationships with key clients.

4.4 Were promoted or seconded

Recall examples of where you may have deputised for a manager, received a promotion, secondments or were headhunted/approached to work for a company.

Examples:

- Progressed from Sales Executive to Managing Director of ABC Limited over a period of eight years.
- Promoted to Regional Manager within two years of joining; now responsible for managing a team of 80 staff and five units worth £15m per annum.
- Joined XYZ Ltd as a Trainee and was promoted to Assistant Manager within twelve months.

- Performed two simultaneous roles for a six-month period following the departure of the Area Manager.
- Seconded to the US for a twelve-month period to set up international contact centre; recruited, coached and trained a team of seven from scratch and appointed a manager to oversee the operation.

4.5 Demonstrated team working and/or leadership capabilities

Provide details of any projects you may have worked on or managed. Include examples of where you may have been involved in training or supporting staff, and anything that will demonstrate your ability to lead or work as part of a team.

Examples:
- Manage one of the toughest technology departments in ABC plc, which consists of 50 staff based both in London and New York, and 1,200 support staff.
- Acted as a mentor to a number of up-and-coming managers, providing them with comprehensive training on effectively running a unit, which led to ...
- Project managed the successful integration of two trading systems that were implemented with zero downtime or loss to the business.
- Played a fundamental role in developing and growing company from standing start to a team of 25 within an 18-month period.

4.6 Received an award or recognition

Have you received any awards in recognition for a job well done?

Example:
- Nominated for St. Mary's 'Distinguished Teacher's Award in 2007, the highest accolade awarded to teaching staff at all levels within the university.
- Achieved Best UK Engineering Award for 'Skills development

utilising Lean Six Sigma capability'; trained all senior managers in Lean Six Sigma.

4.7 Received a commendation or endorsement

Have you received praise, written or verbal, from a colleague, manager, peer or client? Including one or two recommendations can validate your worth to a company. A commendation can also be presented in quote form just below your profile if particularly impressive or from a well-renowned company or individual.

Example:

"Cay-Leigh is professional and undoubtedly an individual of great integrity. With such a broad set of qualities, she's an asset to the accountancy profession and I would relish the opportunity to work with her again." James Brown, KPMG

4.8 Solved a problem

Employers are interested in how you can solve their problems, so provide demonstrable examples of the issue, your personal involvement in finding a solution and the outcome.

Examples:

- Transformed the business from a loss-making to a profitable enterprise with an annual turnover of £6m; reorganised internal & external sales teams and restructured the entire business which resulted in a 5% headcount reduction.
- Transformed an under-performing teenage magazine from a static pool into a vibrant, financially viable and profitable production; revitalised editorial content and introduced an 'Agony Column'.

4.9 Were proud of an accomplishment

Include anything else you have been particularly proud of, from how you have performed in relation to your peers, to where you have made a positive contribution. Consider examples of where you have gone the extra mile for the business, clients or colleagues.

How to express the information

1. Detail the company name, location and job title. Include start and end dates.
2. Provide a description of the company in one sentence.
3. In no more than three sentences, define what you were brought in to do – the scope of your role, your duties and responsibilities.

Some pointers

- It is sometimes difficult to differentiate between a duty, a responsibility and an achievement. Consider where you have added value or excelled at a certain task or gone above and beyond.
- In some industries, for example sales and operations, it is relatively easy to quantify achievements and provide tangible examples. This can be more challenging in other industries; focus should be on outcomes of your actions and the business benefit.
- Be detailed about your most recent role and less so thereafter. For chronological CVs, it is suggested that you have between five and seven points for your current role and one less for each role thereafter. With hybrid CVs, as you will have quite an in-depth 'Key Skills' section, it is recommended that you have between four and five points for your current role and fewer for earlier positions.
- It is not necessary to provide detailed information about roles held more than 10 years ago. These roles can merely be listed under a heading of 'Early Career' or 'Pre 20XX'.
- Do not include any summer jobs, part-time jobs, temporary work or internships unless particularly relevant to your target position.

- If you have held numerous positions, consider grouping similar ones together.
- Avoid using the word 'responsible' and do your very best to utilise the action words at the end of the book to describe achievements.
- Do not produce a job description. Select the most salient points of what you do on a day-to-day basis and consider what you have achieved in relation to each duty.
- Write in past tense unless you are writing about your current role.
- Focus on positives and avoid drawing attention to weaknesses or anything negative.
- Include what you have done not things that you hope to still do.
- Place your most impressive statements first.
- If you have too many points, include those statements that are most impressive and or most relevant to your target position.

Potential Problems

1. Employment dates

- If you have had short employment gaps, i.e. a few months here and there, omit the month you started and left, so 2016–2019 as opposed to Mar 2016–April 2019.
- Should there be obvious gaps in your employment history consider producing a functional CV.

2. Career breaks

- Time out to have children, travel or take a sabbatical is part of life. Don't be tempted to leave it out and create a glaring gap. Instead, consider what you achieved during this period. Perhaps you project managed a self-build, headed the PTA, or learned a new skill. Recruiters would rather know than not know; eliminate speculation.

3. Job titles

- Keep job titles generic as you need to appeal to as many people as possible.
- To avoid pigeon holing oneself, be specifically vague, for example, instead of junior accountant Level II, just use accountant.

4. Contractor/Consultant

- As a contractor or consultant you may have worked on several short assignments. Contemplate replacing 'Employment History' with 'Recent Projects'/'Selected Projects' or 'Contracting Assignments'. Detail the most relevant projects, showcasing the task, your involvement and the outcome or business benefit. This will ensure you are not viewed as a 'job hopper'.

5. You have only worked for one company

- Provide details of some or all jobs held with the company to show progression. You can also allude to progression when you provide a summary of your duties and responsibilities. Keep the most recent two or three roles separate, any roles thereafter can be summarised or combined if similar.

6. Company information

- If you have worked abroad or for a relatively unknown organisation in the UK, provide a short description of the company. This provides the reader with an understanding of the type and size of organisations you have experience of working for.

7. Sensitive information

- If there is a concern over confidentiality, it is perfectly acceptable to state 'a National Chain' or 'Investment Bank'. The company name can be provided at interview.
- Be careful when it comes to including sensitive company information that is not in the public domain.

Examples of Work History

Below are examples of what can be included in your work history and how to present the information. As with the examples below, the focus should be on what you achieved, and the outcome/result. Where possible, quantify each point.

Example 1:

XYZ Insurance Agency, Hertfordshire   **Feb 2017–Present**

Director and Founder

Set up this business from scratch to provide a range of B2B insurance products. Manage the day-to-day operations including all administration, internal business processes, workflow, policy making and strategy. Regularly negotiate with suppliers thereby securing preferential rates and terms.

- Grew business from standing start; turned over £400k in first year and built team of 25 across all disciplines.
- Secured three major corporate accounts in first six months, winning business previously held by major players in the industry.

Example 2:

XYZ Company, Surrey   **2015–Date**

Manufacturers of road construction and maintenance plant and equipment.

Administration Officer/PA

Recruited to provide secretarial and administrative support to a team of five senior managers.

- Devised and implemented standard processes and procedures on behalf of the administration team, in compliance with company policy.
- Successfully organised three major corporate events including two conferences and an exhibition for up to 500 representatives.

- Improved the servicing and renewal processes which enhanced customer journey; created and maintained an access database to effectively monitor the process.
- Cleared a four-month backlog of invoices.

Example 3:

XYZ IT Company, London   **Feb 2016–Date**

Technical Manager

Appointed to deliver major internet systems to clients across Hertfordshire. Managed several technical teams of up to twenty developers and worked closely with new and existing clients in order to understand their exacting requirements.

- Played a fundamental role in shaping the strategic direction of the department and ensured each technical team adopted best practices and processes to facilitate the smooth technical delivery of each client project.
- Successfully delivered several completed, working and tested projects within agreed timescales and on budget. Provided detailed plans, developed appropriate documentation and produced regular project status reports for each project.
- Acquired two new corporate clients with estimated revenue of £150k following works completed for ...

Example 4:

May 2019 to date: Contracts Manager, ABC Construction, Nottingham

Appointed to maintain accurate records including site diaries, health and safety records and ledgers covering personnel, payroll, supplies and inventory. Compile and submit quarterly P&L reports to senior management. Supervise a team of 30 operative and up to 10 subcontractors.

- Considerably reduced the number of customer complaints; initiated and implemented preventative maintenance, improving client relations.
- Seconded to XYZ Ltd for a period of six months to turnaround this under-performing concern. Implemented operational procedures and restructured departments, which saw each business unit meeting targets and achieving margins for the first time in 18 months.

Example 5:
If you have held more than one position with the same company express as follows:

XYZ Company, London   Aug 2015–Date

Sales Manager   Mar 2016–Date
Promoted within a few months of joining to manage, train, motivate and develop a team of six field representatives.
- Identified new business opportunity worth a potential £1m per annum; regularly monitored market trends and competitor activity.
- Introduced a new product, diversifying business activities and increasing company revenue by 10% in the first six months of its introduction.
- Achieved a 20% increase in revenue in first eight months; maintained positive customer relationships through adopting a consultative sales approach.
- Commended by Sales Director as team consistently met or exceeded targets for six consecutive months, a first for the business.

Field Representative   Aug 2015–Feb 2016
- Sold an extensive range of corporate FMCG merchandise to SME clients across the UK. Increased the number of new enquiries to the business by 20% and secured over 50 new accounts.

- Increased conversion rates by 42%.
- Praised for consistently achieving targets and meeting business objectives.
- Developed a customer database to analyse buying patterns and individual customer requirements, in order to deliver a tailor-made service.

Spend some time detailing your 'Work History' for the last decade. Focus on STAR (Situation, Task, Action and Result) and utilise the action words at the end of this book.

Skills-based/Functional CVs

This section should be entitled 'Career Summary'. As the intention of a functional CV is to detract from your career history, all that is required is a summary of your work history experience.

Compiling the content

Write down all the positions you have held starting with the most recent. Detail the company name, location, start and end dates for each one.

Some Pointers

- Ensure there are no gaps in your career history. Incorporate travel, career breaks or secondments.
- If you have had several job or temporary positions:
  - group similar jobs;
  - avoid using months on your CV, just the year you commenced and left.
- Keep job titles generic as you need to appeal to as many people as possible.
- List your roles in reverse chronological order, i.e. most recent first.

Examples

Example 1:

2020–Date	**Career Break: Part-time studies and Travel**
2016–2020	**XYZ Company, London**
2018–2020	*Regional Sales Manager*
2016–2018	*Area Manager*
2014–2016	**ABC Limited, Edinburgh**
	Assistant Account Manager
2010–2014	**DCT plc, London**
	Client's Assistant
2005–2010	**Various Contracts** (Deutche Bank, Coutts, J P Morgan)

Example 2:

ABC Ltd, London	**2017–Date**
Customer Service Officer	
Career Break: Full-time Mother	**2016–2017**
DGH plc, London	**2013–2015**
Marketing Consultant	
PQR Ltd, London	**2010–2012**
Claims Advisor	
XYX Ltd, London	**2008–2010**
Office Accounts Junior	

Example 3:

2016–Date **General Sales Manager: IXY Drinks Company,** Surrey

2014–2016 **Export Sales Manager: MXY plc,** London

2012–2014 **Area Sales Manager/Sales Associate: Various**

2010–2012 **Telesales: DEG Limited,** Hertfordshire

Pre-2010 **Early career in Accountancy**

Example 4:

2017–Date **Social Host, ABC Limited:** London

2015–2017 **Croupier, CDA Limited:** Portsmouth

2011–2014 **Waitress/Bartender, XYZ Ships:** Portsmouth

2009–2011 **Personal Assistant, XYZ plc:** London

CHAPTER 11

Voluntary Work

Offering your services as a volunteer not only assists your community and allows you to help others, but it can enrich your life and work experience. Voluntary work or unpaid work experience can also bolster your CV as it demonstrates commitment and a willingness to learn. This is even more so if you have gained experience that is directly relevant to your target position.

When to Include Voluntary Work on Your CV

For entry-level jobseekers, it is recommended that you divulge all employment, voluntary or otherwise. Voluntary work can empower young people, instil confidence and self-awareness amongst other skills, and this will be of interest to a prospective employer.

For the more experienced jobseeker, include voluntary work if it will be supportive to your application and/or relevant to your target position. Voluntary work can tell a prospective employer a lot about you as an individual; it may very well add credibility to your application, and it is more often than not seen in a very positive light.

'Most employers will expect to see some kind of voluntary work on your CV, demonstrating how you have given your time either to help those less fortunate or to help develop your profession or work area. Discretion would be advisable if this work is in a controversial area or is a deeply polarising issue (such as Brexit).'

ROBIN WEBB, PRINCIPAL CV CONSULTANT AT CV MASTER CAREERS

Where to include examples

Include voluntary work as part of your work history if it forms a good chunk of your experience and is particularly relevant to your career, or as a subheading under 'Additional Information' at the end of your CV. Or, include as a separate section after work history.

Example 1:

- Voluntary work: A qualified Mountain Leader who regularly organises various outdoor pursuits for groups of children.

Example 2:

Jan 2019–July 2019 XYZ School, Class Room Assistant

As a volunteer, two days per week, provided support to the Head of English, supervising the class in her absence.

- Offered help to children struggling with reading or learning difficulties.
- Prepared classes and planned several activity sessions.

Example 3:

- Voluntary work: Raised circa £500k over a three-year period; co-ordinated and planned several fundraising initiatives each year for XYZ Charity.

Example 4:

Volunteer   **2015–2017**

- Organised two fundraising events, which combined, raised £5,000. Utilised the funds to set up a crèche, which benefited 10 families and 22 children.
- Designed and created a company website for a not-for-profit organisation; developed all the content, organised hosting and identified potential partners.

CHAPTER 12

Professional Associations/Memberships

As per Wikipedia, a professional association or professional society is: *'an organisation, usually non-profit that exists to further a particular profession, to protect both the public interest and the interests of professionals'.*

Professional bodies are often involved in developing and monitoring professional educational programs, updating skills and perform professional certification to denote that a person possesses qualifications in the subject area. Membership of a professional body is sometimes synonymous with certification. In some professions, membership of a professional body can form the primary formal basis for gaining entry to and setting up practice within the profession.

Not everyone will be a member of or belong to a professional, regulatory or student body. Listing your membership shows dedication to you career, if relevant to your chosen vocation.

Do not include religious or political associations; a CV is a representation of your professional, not your personal life.

How to Present the Information

Should a professional membership be relevant to your career, it can be detailed in one of five places:

- List the professional affiliations and credentials after your name at the top of your CV.
- Profile section: allude to it in your profile statement if it's particularly relevant to your career.
- Education: include as part of your Education and Qualifications.

- Separate section below Education: opt for a separate section should you have three or more memberships to list.
- Under a subheading in the 'Additional Information' section at the end of your CV.

This section can be entitled 'Professional Affiliations', 'Professional Associations' or 'Memberships'. Include the name of the organisation, acronym (if appropriate), followed by the date you became a member.

Examples:

Member of the British Institute of Innkeeping (MBII) 2016–Date

Associate Chartered Institute of Bankers (ACIB) since 2016

Member of the Institute of Operations Management (IOM) since 2013

Associate member of the Institute of Management Consultants 2019

Member of the British Computer Society 2017

Fellow of the Institute of Sales and Marketing Management (UK) 2016

Professional member of the Chartered Institute of Personnel & Development (CIPD), 2017

Publications and Patents

This section will not be relevant to everyone. Publications and/or patents only need to be included if relevant to your target position.

Listing Publications

When listing publications, the following should be noted:

1. Have separate headings for:
    (a) Publications – with sub-heading Articles, Book Contributions and Reviews (if appropriate);
    (b) Research Papers;
    (c) Courses and Conferences Attended;
    (d) Teaching Experience.

2. List in reverse chronological order, i.e. most recent first.

3. Indicate authors according to original order and indicate the first and last page of the article.

4. Detail the full name of the article or paper, and the date it was published.

5. Include a URL if available online.

Where to include

In a separate section after 'Education', detail relevant publications. State 'more information on publications is available on request'. Academics should consider an appendix.

Listing Patents

When listing a patent, specify whether the patent has been granted or is pending, the patent number, and the country in which it was awarded.

Where to include

In a separate section after 'Education' and 'Professional Memberships'.

CHAPTER 14

Computer/Technical Skills

Computers are an essential part of the commercial environment, so regardless of your background or specialisation, it is imperative that you are computer literate. Whether you have an official qualification or are self-taught, add detail of your proficiency with various packages, systems or programming languages.

Non-technical and technical backgrounds are discussed separately.

Non-technical Backgrounds

Under 'Additional Information', the last section of your CV, add the subheading 'IT Skills'. In no more than two lines, describe your proficiency with each package or system.

Examples

Example 1:
- Fully conversant with Microsoft Office to an advanced level; familiar with the mechanics of web design.
- Experienced with various operating systems including Windows, XP, MAC and Dos.

Example 2:
- Proficient user of Microsoft Office – Word, Excel, Access, PowerPoint and Outlook.
- Basic understanding of databases including SQL server, My SQL and ORACLE.

Example 3:

- Highly competent user of Microsoft Word, Excel, Access and Publisher.
- Proficient in various programming languages including Microsoft Visual Fox Pro6 and J2EE, and web technologies including Java Script and Dreamweaver MX.

Should you be responding to a specific position where you are expressly required to have experience with a certain package or system, allude to it in your profile statement or key skills section.

Technical Backgrounds

This section is for those with a technical background or those seeking a role in IT. Under the title of 'Technical Skills', 'IT Skills', or 'Technical Competencies', provide a detailed breakdown of your technical competencies.

How to present the information

The amount of detail provided and the way the information is expressed, will be dependent on your experience and on what technical skills you are looking to highlight. This section can be presented in one of three ways:

Example 1:

- Border Gateway Protocol (BGP)/Multi-protocol BGP (MP-BGP).
- TCP/Ipv4: OSPF, IS-IS, EIGRP and all other IGPs. TCP/Ipv6: all current protocols.
- WAN/LAN: DSL, ATM, FR, ISDN, VPN, VOIP, GSR/XR, C6500, C3750/3550,CSS11500, ASA/PIX.
- Cisco Wireless networks 4404 Controllers, 1xxx series Aps and all Cisco Wireless Management software.
- MCSE NT4.0, MCSD, A+, Windows (Vista, XP and 2003), Office 2003, Linux and Unix (freeware versions).

- Vmware, Checkpoint, HP-Openview, CiscoWorks, Spectrum, Remedy, Smarts, Rancid, Vital Suite, MRTG/Perl and Websense.

Example 2:

Desktop Operating Systems MS-DOS v3.x – v6.x, Windows 3.x – XP, Linux (SuSe, Ubuntu OpenLinux)

Network Operating Systems Windows Server v4.0 – 2003, Novell Netware v3.x –v5.x, Vmware (Workstation/GSX Server)

Messaging Lotus Notes/Domino 4.x/5.x/6.x Server, Exchange 5.5 –2003, Outlook 97 – XP. Blackberry Server v3.x/4.x

LAN/WAN Technology Switches (Cisco, 3Com, HP), Routers (Cisco 2600, 2500, 1700, 1600) Protocols – IPX/SPX, TCP/IP (DNS, DHCP) Cabling – 1000BaseT, 100BaseT, 10BaseT, Fibre PIX Firewall (520,515)

Software Packages Microsoft Office, Lotus SmartSuite, Adobe, Macromedia, Corel desktop applications Various Anti-Virus solutions – Dr Solomon's, McAfee Disk Imaging/cloning – Ghost 4/5, Drivecopy Helpdesk Software: Quetzal/Utopia/Infoman/ Netman Backup Software: Arcserve, Brightsor, Tapeware Remote Control Software: PcAnywhere, CarbonCopy, NetOp, VNC, Remote Desktop

Scripting Languages Vbscript, HTML, Pascal, Qbasic

Example 3:

If space is an issue, your technical skills can be expressed as follows:

- *Project* • *Siebel Sytems* • *Oracle OSO* • *Dos*
- *Clarify Clear Sales* • *Visio* • *Windows 3.1* • *Windows 95/97/98/00* • *Frame relay/IP WAN technology*

Where to present the information

If you are seeking a managerial role, this section can be placed after employment history.

If you are seeking a more technical role where your technical skills will be of great interest to a prospective employer, this section should come directly after 'Key Skills' or if not applicable, directly after your 'Profile' on page one of your CV.

CHAPTER 15

Languages

With many companies having global operations, organisations are often looking for candidates with multi-cultural experience and foreign language skills. As such, it is important to provide details of your proficiency with a language whether it be basic, conversational or fluent but only if relevant to the job you are applying for.

Compiling This Section

Under 'Additional Information' with a sub-heading of 'Languages', detail your proficiency. Below are some terms that can be used to express your competency:

- Basic knowledge of . . .
- Fluent in . . .
- Conversational . . .
- Read, write and understand . . .
- Native English speaker fluent in . . . with basic . . . language skills
- Good understanding of . . .
- Advanced Spanish and basic French language skills
- Fluent in German (mother-tongue) and English
- Multilingual: fluent in English, Spanish, Russian and French
- Bilingual: French and English

When applying for a role where there is a language requirement, emphasise the language skill in your 'Profile Statement' or 'Key Skills' section.

Additional Information

This section is used to express any other information that may be of interest to a potential employer including driving status, willingness to travel, interests and hobbies, any roles in the military, obligations on a personal level, honours, awards, nominations, sporting interests or achievements, language skills, IT skills, voluntary work or anything else that will add value to your application. Keep it relevant.

Personal information such as date of birth, marital status, nationality and number of dependents should not be included as per Government legislation and the Age Discrimination Act 2006. It provides no bearing on your ability to do the job.

Information That Can Be Included

1. Drivers licence

Include your driving status if the job you are applying for states that you should hold a specific type of driving licence or if your job is likely to involve travel. Provide details of what licence you hold and in the case of car licence, whether your licence is 'full and clean'. If not clean, i.e. you have points on your licence, state 'full'.

Examples of specialist driving licences:
- Class C and C&E LGV Truck Driving Licence.
- Motorcycle and HGV C+E.
- C1 Licence.
- LGV1 entitlement.

2. Location
Should you be 'willing to relocate or travel', express this here.

3. Security clearance
If your career requires an active or current security clearance, include this here or make mention of it in your 'Profile Statement'.

Examples of Security Clearance Requirements:
- Secret (S).
- Sensitive Compartmentalised Information (TS/SCI I).
- NSA or CIA.
- Top Secret (TS).
- Cleared to work on Restricted and Confidential Government Systems.
- Achieved high security clearance.

4. Interests and hobbies
It is open to interpretation as to whether this section should be included. The consensus from most of the experts interviewed was:
- If you do include hobbies and/or interests, keep them as relevant as possible.
- Do not incorporate something you did just once.
- Keep it to no more than one or two sentences; do not go on for half a page.
- Avoid including social activities that people are likely to make a judgement on, such as shooting or religion.
- Do not include the stereotypical interests such as 'walking, reading and swimming'.

A prospective employer can tell a lot about a person from their interests and/or hobbies, and having them on a CV can serve as an icebreaker and break down barriers at interview.

'It brings personality to what can otherwise be a mundane document. You never know what the recruiter or hiring manager might be looking out for and one of your specialist interests or hobbies might be spot on, just right for other projects or plans they know about. But if it's on your CV, be prepared to talk about it. If you attended a karate lesson 10 years ago, it's not a hobby.'
DANIELL MORRISEY, SENIOR EDITORIAL EARLY CAREERS SCHEMES MANAGER AT THE BBC

'It helps me visualise what sort of person they are. I think interests and hobbies are actually quite important as it shows people have a balance in life; some people don't have any interests and hobbies and again, that says something about the individual.'
GILES CREWDSON, PARTNER AT CREWDSON AND PARTNERS

'We have found a shift towards employers wanting a little more focus on what people do outside of work. Consider providing a few lines on interesting hobbies or activities outside of work. This can help employers see how you de-stress, manage your mental health and give an insight into the type of person you are.'
ROBIN WEBB, PRINCIPAL CV CONSULTANT AT CV MASTER CAREERS

In my view, this is your one and only opportunity to add something personal to your CV, so exploit it. If your interests and hobbies relate directly to what you do or help demonstrate certain skills such as organisation or leadership, they are worth including.

'Interests which are linked to the profession should be included. So, if I have somebody apply for a marketing job, I would like to know whether they are involved with any professional bodies, whether they have participated in international conferences and whether they have written any articles. This is very important because it shows that it is not only a job that they are looking for, it's much more than that; it's a passion, it's something they believe in, it's really their career.'

ADRIAN COJOCARU, DIRECTOR AT TABERNAM SKINNER LTD

5. Extra-curricular activities

Extracurricular activities are simply something you do outside of a paying job. They range from academic, arts and music through to being part of a club.

Entry-level job seekers should consider activities that highlight teamwork, leadership skills, drive and enthusiasm.

Examples – Additional Information

Example 1:

Driving Licence:	Full
Location:	Willing to travel
Languages:	Fluent in French and German
Interests:	Enjoy technology, keeping up-to-date with financial affairs, skiing and spending time with family

Example 2:

Security Clearance:	Cleared to SC Level
Location:	Willing to relocate
IT Skills:	Proficient with Microsoft Office
Interests:	Web design, socialising and keeping fit

CHAPTER 17

References

Providing references on your CV is an area of contention. Most experts agree references should be provided after interview stage so unless you are explicitly asked to provide them, it is recommended you omit them from your CV.

The risk of providing references is that there is nothing to stop a prospective employer contacting your current employer, who is likely to be unaware that you are in the market for a new job.

An added benefit to providing references after interview stage is that you have time to request permission from your referees and are also able to brief them on the position and the skills required to perform the job.

It is quite acceptable, space permitting, to put 'references available on request'.

CHAPTER 18

Layout, Presentation, Structure and CV Design

Layout, presentation, structure and CV design are almost as important as the content itself. If your CV is not visually appealing and well written, it may be passed over. Consider using one of the online templates provided but if you do opt to go it alone, it is worth reading this chapter to ensure you get it right, as first impressions really do count. Templates are hosted on www.theCVdoctor.co.uk (see 'How to use this book' section on p.xix for details on how to access).

'You never get a second chance to make a first impression.'
MATT LAUER

CV writing is an art form but art can be copied. The art is to include enough information to keep your audience captivated but at the same time not to provide too much detail, so as to lose their interest.

'CVs are sales documents; they should leave the reader wanting more. If you give the whole story, people will make a view – they will make a judgement, maybe the right one, maybe the wrong one.'
GILES CREWDSON, PARTNER AT CREWDSON & PARTNERS

A CV should be clear, concise, focused, well structured and easy to read.

This chapter covers correct layout, presentation, how to structure the information and format selection.

Layout

Position the most relevant information on the first page and in order of importance. Generally, those with less than two years' work experience will look to highlight their education as this will be of most interest to a potential employer. Those with more experience will look to highlight areas of expertise and employment history. As mentioned in individual chapters, if you are applying for a specific job and need to draw attention to maybe your technical expertise or language skills, these should be presented on page one of your CV.

Do not begin your CV with information that is out of date, i.e. qualifications completed in 1975. Present the information in reverse chronological order, i.e. most recent first.

Finally, do not be tempted to write your CV as a story as this makes your CV difficult to read.

The standardised sequence of a CV is as follows:

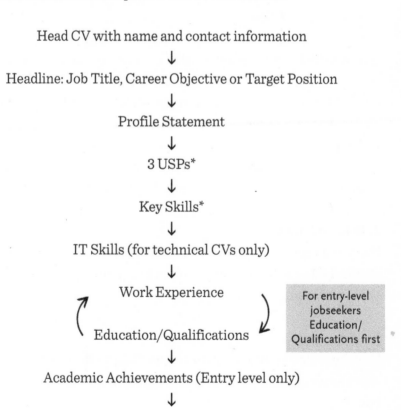

Head CV with name and contact information
↓
Headline: Job Title, Career Objective or Target Position
↓
Profile Statement
↓
3 USPs*
↓
Key Skills*
↓
IT Skills (for technical CVs only)
↓
Work Experience
Education/Qualifications
↓
Academic Achievements (Entry level only)
↓

For entry-level jobseekers Education/Qualifications first

Professional Memberships

↓

Publications/Patents

↓

Additional Information

(such as languages, IT skills, Voluntary work, hobbies and interests)

*More likely for those with 2+ years of experience

Presentation

The importance of presentation should not be underestimated. Your CV communicates your skills, assets and hire-ability, and should therefore project professionalism. This section examines how to create a reader-friendly document that is appealing to the eye.

1. Font type and size

Selecting the right font and size makes a real difference. Recruiter-approved fonts, which are scannable and easy to read, are a serif or sans serif font such as Arial, Tahoma, Calibri, Times New Roman, Verdana, Cambria, Garamond, Book Antiqua, Trebuchet MS or Didot. If a recruiter cannot read your words due to the use of a funky font, your CV will be passed over.

Font size should range between 9 and 12 points, with a larger font size of 18-22 points for your name and 14-16 points for headings.

2. Bold and italics

Use italics and bold to highlight certain areas or key points, but use sparingly. Too much of something can become over-bearing and can appear arrogant.

3. White space

To ensure that your document is appealing to the eye, utilise lots of white space and allow for margins of at least 2cms on the top, sides and bottom.

4. Consistency

Consistency is key. Here are some things to be aware of:

- **Spacing:** spacing between lines and paragraphs should be the same throughout.
- **Font size:** font type and size must be consistent.
- **Dates:** align dates on the right-hand side and if you use full month, i.e. June, do not abbreviate September to Sep.
- **Style:** style should be uniform. For example, all company names capitalised and company descriptions written in italics.
- **Money:** when mentioning money, be consistent in denominations – use £2m rather than £2million and use a lower case m throughout.

5. Bullet points

Utilise bullet points throughout as it makes your document reader-friendly and it's easy on the eye.

6. Complex formatting

As with fancy fonts, it is tempting to use colour, borders, shading, tables and graphics to help you stand out. Coloured headings work but complex formatting can interfere with ATS. Simplicity is best.

7. Headings

Utilising headings makes your CV look clean, reader friendly and easy to follow. Keep your headings consistent in appearance, i.e. same font and size, and place them in capitals and bold.

8. Spelling and grammar

A well-written, error-free CV is vital if you want to sell yourself effectively. Spelling mistakes, poor grammar and typos are surprisingly common and are a bug bear of many recruiters/hiring authorities. These error types can be one of the most serious mistakes you can make; it displays a lack of attention to detail and can result in your CV being binned. Triple check your spelling and grammar.

'I would never ever expect to see a typo in a CV; so if spelling is not a strength, get someone to proofread for you.'

ANNA TOMKINS, HEAD OF TALENT AND RESOURCING AT VODAFONE

9. Format

A Word document is the preferred format for most employers/ recruitment professionals. Whilst PDF files are the best at preserving the design and format of your CV, Word is also the most ATS-friendly file type.

10. Other formatting considerations

Use full stops at the end of every sentence. When using numbers, numbers ten and below should be written in full and numerals from 11 onwards. Money should always be expressed in figures. Text should be justified.

Tip

When emailing your CV make sure you pay as much attention to your email as you did to your CV.

Formatting tips

- keep it simple;
- use bullet points throughout;
- avoid gimmicks, logos and fancy fonts;
- keep it organised;
- ensure the layout is easy on the eye;
- dates should line up;
- fonts type and size should be consistent;
- do not overuse bold;
- use headings;
- avoid producing a monologue.

Your CV is your marketing document and says a lot about you as an individual. If the content has been poorly presented in any way, you can be assured that the prospective employer will build an image of you in their mind and will make a judgement, rightly or wrongly, about you as a prospective employee.

Structure

This section covers how to structure the information and discusses the ideal CV length.

Selling points

Ensure that key points jump out on your CV.

'You shouldn't make the reviewer work too hard to find your crown jewels; if you have three or four key selling points, whatever they might happen to be, it's imperative to make sure that those are very much in evidence on the page.'

JONATHAN JONES, HEAD OF TALENT AT ROIVANT PHARMA

Keep your target audience in mind when writing your CV as selling points may vary depending on the role being applied for.

'People need to adjust their message depending on the role or the company. Be very focused on whom you are targeting and deliver on the target.'

ADRIAN COJOCARU, DIRECTOR AT TABERNAM SKINNER LTD

Sentences and paragraphs

- Sentences need to be kept short and punchy, making it easy to read. Vary your sentence length and keep sentences to no more than 15 words.
- Do not use three words when one will do.
- Keep paragraphs to no longer than four lines.

Language

- CVs should always be written in the first person, for example, 'I have' rather than 'he has'. Ideally the 'I' should be omitted altogether.
- Avoid jargon unless you work in a highly technical field. Your CV needs to appeal to the widest possible audience.
- Do not include job titles and company-specific jargon that will not be understood outside of your company.
- Stay away from obscure words.
- Avoid abbreviations in your CV unless you are expressing your education or professional affiliations.
- Vary your words and phrases as repetition reduces the impact of your CV.

CV Length

Ideally, an experienced jobseeker's CV should be two pages whilst an entry-level job seeker's CV should be just one. Medical, academic and technical CVs can be longer.

'Two pages are more than enough because you want to provide enough information to get the interest of the recruiter and then use the interview to build on the skills and behaviour required for the role.'
SEAN JOWELL, PRODUCTS MD RECRUITMENT LEAD FOR EUROPE AT ACCENTURE

'Two pages are ideal, although if it could fit on to one page, even better. What is important is the quality of the information.'
ADRIAN COJOCARU, DIRECTOR AT TABERNAM SKINNER LTD

'More is less. If you are speaking to people who have an understanding of the industry that you have worked in, [providing a lot of detail] can be patronising to the reader.'
GILES CREWDSEN, PARTNER AT CREWDSON & PARTNERS

Summary

- Divide information into clear, easy to read sections. The use of headings is important.
- Place the most important information on the first page.
- Provide enough information to whet the reader's appetite and ensure that you leave them wanting more.
- Keep the information structured, concise and relevant.

CV Design

You have the choice to opt for a simple, text-led design or a graphical, more complex one. Simple can appear boring and it can be hard for you to stand out, but, in my opinion, the benefits outweigh the risks. A simple design allows you to provide good detail, it offers clear lines, it is visually appealing, easy to follow and it is compatible with ATS systems. To allow you to make an informed decision, let's explore graphical CVs in more detail.

A graphical CV is an evolution of the more traditional CV. Rather than black text and simple formatting, a trend has begun to move towards the use of a more 'design-led' document. These designs can incorporate 'side-bars' or 'skills graphs' to represent skill level/experience in things like software packages. These CVs also tend to be one page.

Robin Webb, Principal CV Consultant at CV Master Careers, believes that the graphical format is set to continue and is becoming more widely accepted. There are some key advantages over the more traditional, 'text-led' approach.

Advantages

- Improved visual impact which helps set you apart from the crowd.
- An opportunity to display individuality and creativity as there is a huge range of designs and colours available.

- Recruiter-friendly as a graphical representation is quicker to 'read' than a paragraph or bullet point.
- Demonstrates technical capabilities as they require technical knowhow to assemble.
- On trend as they are evolving.
- Require less space as only one page.

Whilst Robin's views are that a well-presented graphical CV can be much more effective at helping you beat the competition, there are some common pitfalls.

Drawbacks

- The format is not accepted by all recruiters. Some view them as 'gimmicky'.
- Formats are restrictive (less room for text) and hence they are not suitable for all experience levels. It is difficult to convey the level of detail required for senior or very technical candidates.
- There is no standard format for presenting the information which means recruiters need to spend time 'translating' graphical information. For example, you may state that your skill level for Microsoft Excel is 4 out of 5. How does that compare to someone who describes their Excel skills as advanced with an ability to use functions and formulas?
- Graphical information cannot be read by ATS which is an issue as almost all recruiters/employers use ATS. With careful design selection, sufficient keyword density can still be achieved.
- Poor template selection results in a restrictive format which means it can be hard for the finished product to look good.
- Digital format can be problematic. It is imperative that the document opens and displays correctly so the final product should be produced in PDF format. PDF, however, does not always perform well with ATS.

Summary

There are some distinct advantages to using a graphical CV design but at present, there are several drawbacks too. Select the CV design that you are most comfortable with. You will quickly know whether it is working for you and can always revert to the other.

Tip

Select a professional file name. Best practice is 'First Name Last Name CV MMYY' rather than 'My CV (Best One)'.

CHAPTER 19

Reviewing Real CVs

This chapter provides examples of CVs from real people, each of whom was receiving a poor response to their CV. The examples provided cover a variety of industries and include people at different stages in their career.

Reading through each individual's original CV and the detailed commentary, will help you identify common mistakes and point out 'how not' to write a CV.

In each instance, the revised, professionally-reformatted CV is provided.

Example 1: James Dean
James is a senior marketing professional seeking to secure a Senior Marketing or Business Development role.
Example 2: Amelia White
Amelia is an Architect seeking to secure a position abroad.
Example 3: Andrea Smith
Andrea is a highly qualified graduate and first-time job seeker seeking to secure a position within a consultancy.
Example 4: Leann King
Leann is an experienced Teaching Assistant seeking to secure a new role as she is relocating.
Example 5: Alan Jones
Alan is a Senior Manager with more than 20 years' experience in operations, manufacturing and in the deployment of major production initiatives.

<u>**Curriculum Vitae**</u>

James Dean

Location: Chandler's Ford, Hampshire | Telephone: 07903 000 000 | Email jdean@gmail.com

<u>Professional profile</u>

I am a confident and experienced marketing account director and business development professional currently working within the property sector but seeking a new and challenging account management and business development opportunity.

<u>Core skills</u>

- Managing client and key stakeholder relationships
- Interpretation of the client's needs to fulfil the brief with a view to exceeding the client's expectations
- Conceiving and managing the creation of creative marketing solutions for clients.
- Managing the in-house design, digital and visualisation teams to create digital and creative marketing assets for clients
- Facilitating the design, production and installation of hoardings and signage to promote property developments
- Creative management of sub-contractors including photographers, videographers, installation teams
- Significant product development expertise, promoting brands through brochure design, packaging design, product labels and point of sale
- Management of production and installations for show homes and marketing suites for clients.
- Team leadership and support, a 'team player'
- Excellent communication and networking skills

<u>Career summary</u>

2012 to present   **Templeton Marketing**

Account Marketing Director

Successfully delivered and managed branding, marketing and production solutions for a variety of clients predominantly in the property development sector. Responsible for client sourcing, management and retention.

The customer base included some of the UK's largest housebuilders and contractors including Mansion Homes, Superior Homes, Northcliff Homes, Swift Homes, Tiger Construction and Wright & Wright Construction.

2008 to 2012   **24/7 Marketing**

Account Marketing Manager

Conceived and created original solutions focusing on point of sale and packaging solutions for a range of FMCG clients resulting in enhanced POS performance with a measurable uplift in sales volumes during promotional periods.

Clients included Swiss Cottage, Blue Water Ltd, Rich Fox and SmartSteps.

1992 to 2008   **CVV Creative**

Marketing Administrator & Executive

Supported account handlers in the creation of and management of branding, graphic design and creative services for clients across a multitude of industries including the rebrand of Swift Lines from Square Boxes.

Education and qualifications

1994 6 GCSE's

References available on request

Commentary – James Dean

- HEADING – James' CV has been correctly headed with his name and contact details. He uses the title 'Curriculum Vitae'; this is unnecessary as it should be obvious what the document is.

- VISUAL LAYOUT – There needs to be a balance between too much white space and the lack of white space which creates a feeling of clutter and disorganisation. In James' case, there is too much which leaves his CV feeling bare and lacking in content.

- STRUCTURE – The structure could be improved. Page one comprises several bullets used to highlight 'Key Skills'. Limit these to a maximum of seven so you don't lose your reader. Paragraphs are a good length but some sentences, at three lines, are too long-winded.

- LENGTH – James' CV is too short at 1.5 pages which does not supply the reader with enough information. Someone of his experience and level should aim for a full two-page CV.

- ENGLISH LANGUAGE – James' command of the English language is good and there are no spelling or grammatical errors.

- PROFILE – James' profile statement has no 'wow' factor. The focus should be on his experience, areas of strength and why he is the best candidate for the job.

- CORE SKILLS – This section has some key words but it has not been optimised for ATS. At his level, we want a more powerful

list of 'Key Skills' that would match up to a job description.
- CAREER SUMMARY – James' last eight years of experience is summarised in two points, the second of which tells the reader who the company's clients are and nothing else. Emphasis should be on what he has achieved in each of his roles and the business benefit of hiring him.
- EDUCATIONAL HISTORY – This section is brief and to the point.
- ADDITIONAL INFORMATION – It would be nice to see IT skills or something personal like hobbies and interests.

This is a classic example of someone who is underselling themselves. If you make it past the profile, you will have a brief understanding of James' experience and what he has to offer but you will be left feeling underwhelmed.

After working with James', I was able to delve into his achievements and understand the impact he had made on the businesses and clients he had worked with/for. I completed his CV on a Monday and by Thursday the following week, James received and accepted a job offer. His revised CV can be found on the next page.

JAMES DEAN

CHANDLERS FORD | SO53 4SX | TEL: 07903 000000 | EMAIL: JDEAN@GMAIL.COM

BUSINESS DEVELOPMENT / MARKETING MANAGER

SALES | MARKETING | BUSINESS DEVELOPMENT | ACCOUNT MANAGEMENT

Proactive, creative **BDM & Marketing Professional** with 20+ years' experience managing and developing client and key stakeholder relationships across a range of sectors including FMCG, property and construction. An impressive track record of conceiving and managing the creation of sales and marketing solutions for well-known brands including **Swiss Cottage Company, Swift Lines, and Mansion Homes.**

AREAS OF EXPERTISE:

- **Manages entire creative process of a project** from accurately interpreting client brief and presenting ideas through to briefing resource and final delivery.
- **Skilled team leader with a proven ability to lead key projects including full rebrands and promotional campaigns;** effectively utilises resource from across the business to deliver projects on time and within budget.
- **Wealth of experience across the full marketing mix end-to-end** from product development, print, brochure design, packaging, and point-of-sale, through to working on TV commercials, model shoots, brand promotion and PR.

KEY SKILLS

Marketing Solutions	Account Management	Team Leadership
Project Management	Relationship Management	Presentation Skills
Re-Branding	Business Development	Exhibitions & Shows
Research	Stakeholder Management	Client Briefings
Product Development	Networking	Referral Business

PROFESSIONAL EXPERIENCE

TEMPLETON MARKETING, EASTLEIGH   2012 – MAR 2020

Property marketing specialists focused on creating marketing solutions for estate agents, new homes developers and other property industry clients designed to help them sell more property. £3.2M annual turnover with 13 employees.

MARKETING DIRECTOR

Hired as Marketing Manager and was promoted to Marketing Director within 1.5 years. Managed and delivered branding, marketing, and production solutions for a variety of clients predominantly in the property development sector. Oversaw the sales team, 3D department and studio; attended exhibitions, networking and property shows.

- **Launched Express Sands, a Cyprian holiday resort, into the British market.** In collaboration with team, organised several property shows and exhibitions locally and abroad, which led to the sale of all holiday homes.
- **Single-handedly managed rebrand of Tiger Construction, a year-long project.** Facilitated the design, production, installation and continuous management of own branded hoardings and property signage across all their sites.
- **Secured £200K project for Consign,** Manchester's largest construction company. The company were seeking to diversify into property development; managed full rebrand to Bird Estates, including creation of website, brochures, and site maps.
- **Managed brand and launch of a Mansion Homes development in Colchester, a four-year build comprising 2,500 homes.** In collaboration with a single team member, oversaw production of all CGIs and marketing literature; managed design and installation of marketing suites and hoardings, and the continued maintenance thereof.
- **Led a high-end photoshoot of five £25M+ London penthouse apartments, Sunshine Place, on behalf of Swift Homes;** produced a £500 book-bound brochure aimed at premier end of the market.
- **Oversaw the successful branding of Angel Manor on behalf of Superior Homes, an exclusive development of 25 luxury apartments in Mayfair worth £1.5M+;** produced CGI and all literature so properties could sell off-plan.
- **Won a contract with Smart Steps in 2018,** a supplier of feline supplements. Rebranded the packaging across all nutrition ranges; storyboarded and managed photoshoot in France to promote the brand. The packaging is still used today.

24/7 MARKETING, BRADFORD   2008 – 2012

A forward-thinking marketing agency who embraced 3D imaging to provide high-definition marketing models and design protypes to a wide range of clients. Annual turnover circa £5M with 18 employees.

ACCOUNT MARKETING MANAGER

Hired to create and conceive original solutions focusing on point of sale and packaging solutions for a range of FMCG clients.

- **Secured project to design all duty-free packaging for Blue Water's brand worth £300k p.a.** Produced printed sleeve, in advanced print; designed and sourced a cabin baggage system to cater for a two-bottle promotion that ran for 4+ years.
- **Won project to manage the St Patrick's day Point-of-Sale promotion for ABC Large;** created POS promotional packs for their trade clients across England & Ireland.
- **Worked on various internal creative projects for BigM;** managed projects from brief and promotional photography through to creation of brochures, PR material, and material for sales teams to sell into on-and-off trade markets.
- **Appointed Account Manager for Swift Lines account to manage full rebrand following merger with Square Boxes.**
    - **Facilitated simultaneous sponsorship programmes at Silverstone and Wimbledon, a first-time initiative.** Oversaw branding of eight BigM branches locally; carefully researched, developed, and designed a product that would deliver a strong marketing message without compromising branch security.
    - **Managed team that designed all new artwork required for bank literature** in line with all legal requirements, a 24/7 six-week-project, and again when they relocated to Oxford Street.
- **Selected to work on a complex project for Small X2** which required CGI creation of entire gallery to help determine where to incorporate new exhibits from a space and security perspective.
- **Initiated the creation of a virtual supermarket for SweetsRU using VR technology to increase customer spend;** recognised the need to place expensive products at eye-level to prompt impulse buying.

CVV CREATIVE, LONDON   1992 – 2008

A strategic and creative digital marketing agency with £2M+ turnover and 28 employees.

MARKETING ADMINISTRATOR & EXECUTIVE

Joined as a runner to provide support across the business and assist at major exhibitions. Forged strong relations with brand managers across **Swiss Cottage Company, the company's largest account,** and was **promoted to manage** the account across eight brands, which accounted for **60% of CVV's revenue.**

- **Oversaw design of all artwork and packaging for Swiss Cottage and their Point of Sale (POS)**
- **Managed their entire database which housed all photography and media for the company;** first point of contact for all trade customers.
- **Facilitated production of Swiss Cottage's annual brochure;** sourced product and merchandise necessary to produce POS for all its brands.
- **Invited to manage the promotion of all German Beers for the group, including Drost.** Following the success, built presentation units for the on-trade market from sourcing product all the way through to delivery.
- **Created a series of successful TV campaigns to market BigM** in collaboration with above and below the line agencies.

EDUCATION

---

6 GSCEs

PERSONAL

IT Skills: Fully conversant with MS Office.
Hobbies & Interests: Enjoy travel, sailing, cars, bikes, horse riding and films.

AMELIA WHITE
CURRICULUM
VITAE

80 Seventh Avenue,
Northcliff,
Johannesburg,
2195,
Guateng,
South Africa

T: +27 83 200 3000
E: ameliawhite@gmail.com

LI: linkedin.com/in/ameliawhite21/
Skype: ajdesigns@gmail.com

W: ameliawhite.archi
B: behance.com/ameliawhite.archi
AP: adobeportfolio.com/ameliawhite.archi

PROF. SUMMERY

2017 - PRESENT (3 years)

A Professionally qualified and experienced architect with extensive experience in Architecture and the Built Environment.

Key strengths: conceptual and developmental design, technical drafting, planning strategy, conducting inception, development application, construction and close-out documentation for multi-disciplinary architectural projects.

Other areas include; inception, developing & conceptualising, development application, project managing, documentation and implementing company promotional material.

KEY SKILLS

• Inception (Brief & Concept)	• Graphisoft Archicad 12 - 23
• Development Application	• Unreal Engine: Twinmotion
• Documentation	• Microsoft Excel, Word, PowerPoint, Publisher
• Close-Out	• Apple OSX: Pages, Numbers, Keynote, MovieMaker
• Project & Time Management	• Adobe Suite: Photoshop, In-Design.
• Relationship Management	• Advanced Artistic/ Drafting Skills

CAREER HISTORY

EMPLOYER: A-Z ARCHITECTS
POSITION: PROFESSIONAL ARCHITECT (FREE LANCE)
DATES: 2017 - PRESENT

A-Z Architects is a dynamic practice based on experience and youthful dynamism. The A-Z practice was established in 1977 as Jake West Architects.

Reporting to the Principal Agent, accountable for in-house project management of projects to the value of R40+Mill budget. Clients include: Western Farm Diving Club, Gleneagle Residential Development and Sandpiper Oils HQ.

Develop and present architectural documentation from Inception, Concept, Development Application, Construction Documentation and Close-Out phases that are aligned to project management strategies.

Amelia, an associate of the now titled A-Z firm, has worked closely with multi-disciplinary professional team members on some of A-Zs greatest projects. She works closely with the principal agent throughout all stages a large range of projects from inception to close-out stages including site meetings, site inspections and in-house administrative management. Currently, Amelia is Project Architect for the design of Gleneagle Residential Estate, 25 DF Malan Road Business Park Development, the Western Farm Diving Club and is realising the final close-out and interior design realisation for a residential project in Newcastle alongside the Principal Agent.

a. Assess and evaluate time vs cost strategies with project team.
b. Assess and evaluate planning requirement strategies for development of brief and timeline.
c. Design and planning realisation and deadline requirements.
d. Establishing thought leadership position in the firm, with ability to challenge status quo.
e. Maintain a professional relationship with clients and attend, minute and lead progress, site, and inspection meetings as well as briefings as required.
f. Gaining of insights through immersive fieldwork and research with clients and their environment in order to bring client knowledge and insight into each brief.
g. Developing general architectural presentations including concept presentations, cost and time analysis, marketing analysis etc.
h. Conducting on-going research into technology, energy analysis, material specifications and ensuring information is disseminated to relevant professional team members.
i. Involvement in initial briefing sessions with client to understand and identify the problem or opportunity at hand.
j. Compilation and delivery of client presentations (pitch creative work with confidence and passion).
k. Technical detailing and construction documentation.
l. Attended Graphisoft and Unreal annual training sessions to provide strategic documentation at a publications level.
m. Competition entries.

EMPLOYER: SELF EMPLOYED
POSITION: PROFESSIONL ARCHITECT
DATES: 2017 - PRESENT

Amelia experienced UK design and planning requirements when given an opportunity to redesign a private residence for a first-time home owner client in Hampshire. A single story and 1 bedroom house was redesigned to "up-side-down living" in order to take advantage of the south-north orientation of the solar patterns into the living areas of the home on he first floor.

Working remotely, the client communicated between Amelia as the architect, the planning council and building inspector and neighbours to ensure planning approval. Planning approval was granted and construction documentation was carried further by a professional team and RIBA/ ARB accredited architectural engineer. The project has now been altered slightly by Amelia according to the clients new design requirements and is currently being reviewed by the Hampshire Borough Planning Council.

Amelia also redesigned a private residence that was too accommodate an AirBnB on site in Northriding, Guateng. In order to not gain new coverage, Amelia was tasked with gaining an additional bedroom, more public space and an additional shared bathroom. As well as the planning approval for the above, Amelia had to apply for a relaxation submission to council as the existing staircase was built over the building line. approval was gained from the neighbours and submitted to council.

EMPLOYER: A-Z ARCHITECTS
POSITION: CANDIDATE ARCHITECTURAL TECHNICIAN
DATES: 2013 - 2017 (5 years)

Reporting to the Principal Agent, accountable for in-house project management of projects to the value of R350+Mill budget, ranging between inception, construction and close-out phases. Clients include: Ndima Tradeport, Obama Homes, XYZ University of Dubai, Manor House Residental Development (UAE), Mandiba University of Arts.

Develop and present architectural documentation ranging from Inception, Concept, Development Application, Construction Documentation and Close-Out phases that are aligned to project management strategies.

Amelia White began her association with Jake West in 2013 at A-Z Architects in Johannesburg. After completing Bachelor Degree of Architectural Studies at the University of Cape Town, Amelia began her internship with multi-disciplinary professionals designing a variety of health, residential, industrial, mixed-use, retail, education, office and master planning projects around the Johannesburg Area, and international projects such as the XYZ University of Dubai. She has worked closely team members on some of A-Zs greatest projects, including the successfully completed Obama Homes and North Home projects in Cape Town. She worked closely with the principal agent throughout all stages a large range of projects from inception to close-out stages including site meetings, site inspections and in-house administrative management.

a. Conceptualisation and implementation of Mandiba University of Arts (MUA) Implementation Guide Plan for urban planning strategy.
b. Conceptualisation, implementation and close-out of Obama Home for Disabled Kids. Amelia was Project Architect who supervised the project from concept to close-out under supervision of the Principal Agent.
c. Attended Graphisoft's annual training sessions to provide strategic documentation at a publications level.
d. Analysed details to create meaningful and professional documentation / presentations for to publishers, clients & professional team.

EDUCATION

The ABC Property Development Programme (2020) - *Pending*

Amelia is hoping to be accepted to The ABC Property Development Programme, an intensive two-week course (19 - 31 August 2020) that equips professionals to engage with a full range of disciplines within the commercial property industry. The course is developed and delivered in association with the South African Property Owners Association (SAPOA) and covers property finance, valuation, property law, negotiation, investment, development, marketing and management. Amelia believes that with this prestigious qualification, she will have the ability to provide a strong base in strategic thinking, negotiation, financial management, economics and presentation skills. that will majorly benefit to the company that she works for.

South African Institute of Architects

· Professional Architect Registration (SACAP Professional Examination, 2018).

University of Cape Town, School of Architecture & the Built Environment Masters Degree (M.Arch) in Architecture & the Built Environment, (2017-2019)

· Master's Degree in Architecture & the Built Environment: *Current*
· Completed modules: Architectural Design and Thesis, Law in Architecture, Project Management, Architectural Technology, History of Architecture, Architectural Office Management.

South African Institute of Architects

· Candidate Architectural Technologist Registration (2015)

University of Cape Town, School of Architecture & the Built Environment Bachelor's Degree (B.Arch) in Architecture & the Built Environment, (2010-2013)

· Bachelor's Degree in Architecture & the Built Environment.
· Architectural Design and Theory, Architectural Technology, Building Science, History of Architecture, Visual Communication.

Matric: Damelin College, Johannesburg: (2009)
A Aggregate (English, Afrikaans, Maths, French Art, History, Life Sciences)
Amelia Achieved the Damelin Art Prize.

REFERENCES *Amelia has worked in our practice since May 2013 to the present. Having completed her Bachelor of Architectural Studies in 2012, at the University of Cape Town, she joining the practice and has been involved in a number of projects; from concept design stage, through contract documentation, detail design and project administration.*

These projects have all been varied in scale and complexity from multi-storey developments, to institutional projects and residential projects. Amelia has undertaken all her tasks and anything she has been asked to do, with enthusiasm and commitment.

Her artistic ability and skill has been evident in her aesthetic application to architecture. She has also developed highly proficient computer skills in the combined use of drawing and computer generated architectural applications.

Amelia is a talented and enthusiastic student of architecture; I therefore highly recommend that she complete her studies in order for her to be able to fully realise her potential as one of our country's future architects.
- Jake West of A-Z Architects

I had the privilege of working with Amelia White for approximately six months, from the commencement of her employment at A-Z Architects (6th May 2015), until my own move across to J&J Architects (3rd October 2013). During this period, I found her to be a person of great aptitude and diligence. Amelia added value to a variety of different projects, such as the Obama Homes (healthcare), TJ's Shipping (offices) and House Watson (private residential). Her involvement ranged from conceptual design to technical documentation, and she was also exposed to a degree of contract administration as well.

Specific duties fulfilled by Amelia included the following:
• Conceptual design and presentation.
• Design development, including 3D modelling.
• Technical resolution and documentation thereof.
• Submissions to, and liaising with, local authorities.
• Site meetings, including assisting with contract administration.

Execution of these tasks required the rapid development of Amelia's skill set with regards to software such as Graphisoft ArchiCAD, Adobe Photoshop and Microsoft Office, and it was a pleasure to see her competence grow at such a rate, allowing her to contribute positively to practice productivity within a relatively short period.

In addition to her obvious professional potential, Amelia also demonstrated highly admirable personal characteristics, and is undoubtedly an individual of great integrity. With such a broad set of qualities, she is an asset to the architectural profession, and I would relish the opportunity to work with her again, once she has completed her postgraduate qualification.

- Tom Temple - Principal of Temple Architects

Commentary – Amelia White

- HEADING – Amelia's name and contact details take up a third of the first page which is premium space. There is no need to include a full address; her website and portfolio addresses can also be moved to the end of her CV under 'Additional Information'. Including the words 'Curriculum Vitae' takes up more valuable space.

- VISUAL LAYOUT – The content is not presented in a reader-friendly format. There is too much white space on the left-hand side of the page and only a small margin on the right. Varying font sizes are used and big blocks of colour.
- STRUCTURE – Long paragraphs and a lack of bullet points diminish the impact of her CV.
- LENGTH – At five pages, her CV is far too long; her target should be two-pages.
- ENGLISH LANGUAGE – Although Amelia generally has a good command of the English language, there are some typos and grammatical errors which are a no-no on a CV. She has chosen to write in the third person, which is not recommended.
- PROFILE – Amelia's profile focuses quite heavily on skills. Of more interest is her experience and what she can offer ahead of the competition.
- KEY SKILLS – This section is relatively strong and should be retained.
- CAREER SUMMARY – In her first role, Amelia has specified projects she has worked on but includes no detail of her personal involvement or what she achieved. The reader is provided with a list of responsibilities which appear to have been pasted from a job description. Her second role is better, but too detailed; her third, is similar to the first.
- EDUCATIONAL HISTORY – At a full-page, this section is too detailed; only a few lines are necessary.
- REFEREES – Her final page is taken up some great references and testimonials; these are better suited to her LinkedIn profile. In her revised CV, note how I have included part of a commendation.
- ADDITIONAL INFORMATION – Amelia has not included this section. She could include IT skills and/or hobbies/interests.

This is a typical example of a CV that will not pass the seven second test. It is too wordy and too long. The emphasis is on skills and responsibilities rather than achievements and the reader will be left wondering what she has actually done.

I worked closely with Amelia and was able to draw out her achievements. I think you will agree that the revised CV showcases what a talented, skilled architect she is. This CV helped her to quickly secure three job offers: two in Dubai and one in the UK.

AMELIA WHITE

+27(0) 83 200 300| Northcliff, JHB |AMELIAWHITE@GMAIL.COM

QUALIFIED ARCHITECT

Artistic and skilful professionally **qualified Architect** with strong design skills, time-cased management and **seven years' experience in Architecture & the Built Environment** including international projects in the UK and Dubai. Proven ability to manage multi-disciplinary architectural projects on the forefront of global construction including energy-saving trends and unique designs that benefit the community.

Applied to UCT's intensive **Property & Development Programme** to gain valuable insight into property finance, valuation, property law, negotiation, investment, development, marketing, and management within commercial property industry. Course is developed and delivered in association with the South African Property Owners Association (SAPOA).

Areas of Expertise:

✓ Manages projects of varying scale and complexity from initial brief and sketch design through to contract documentation and delivery, from multi-storey developments through to institutional and residential projects.

✓ Develops, presents and manages architectural and urban planning processes, from inception through to close-out stages in architecture and the built environment.

✓ Compiles and delivers design and construction documentation, and pitches creative work with confidence and passion.

"Amelia is professional and undoubtedly an individual of great integrity. With such a broad set of qualities, she's an asset to the architectural profession and I would relish the opportunity to work with her again." Tom Temple, Principal, Temple Architects

---

KEY SKILLS

Conceptual Design	Developmental Design	Technical Drafting
Strategic Planning	Inception (Brief & Concept)	Development Application
Close-Out Documentation	Project Management	Promotional Material
Relationship Management	Time Management	3D Modelling

EXPERIENCE

AMELIA WHITE ARCHITECT   **2017 – DATE**

Firm focused on managing projects as an Architectural Developer, managing end-to-end process from conception through to final stage development.

FOUNDER / ARCHITECTURAL DEVELOPER

- **Secured £250K contract to redesign private residence of a Hampshire based client from normal to "upside-down" living to take advantage of South-North orientation;** single-handedly managed project remotely from design through to planning approval.

- **As Principal Agent, successfully managed a 12-month project involving total refurbishment of a double-storey residence in Cape Town into a fully operational AirBnB;** worked closely with client, contractors and engineers to deliver project on time and within budget including achieving planning for a 'relaxation submission'.

A-Z ARCHITECTS   **2013 – DATE**

A dynamic, forward thinking architectural practise that manages a full range of project types from Urban through to Industrial. Consists of ten architects and accredited with BEE level 4 status. Published & received recognition for several projects in fields of conservation and architecture.

FREELANCE ARCHITECT   **2017 – DATE**

Following resignation in 2017 to focus on master's degree, contacted to project manage several in-house projects of R60M+. Tasked with development and presentation of architectural documentation from Inception, Concept, Development Application, Construction Documentation and Close-Out phases aligned to project management strategies.

- **Supported Architectural Team on evaluation and successful completion of highly profitable R350M+ Ndima Tradeport project** involving design of a 40,000sqm urban block parking substructure to house 400 cars and a super structure.
  - **Minimised potential site delays** through effective co-ordination of technical detailing prior to construction phase.
  - **Instrumental in delivering project on time and within budget;** provided strong team, time and cost management, and effective leadership between engineers and technical team.
- **Project Architect for R50M Western Farm Diving Club Project involving a substantial 245sqm extension to existing building including bathrooms, locker and function rooms, and storage facilities. Still in design phase.**
  - Provide all technical detailing and graphic marketing material, 2D & 3D.
  - Effective liaison between consultants and client; oversee budget, timeline and project status.
- **Commissioned to design three ±450sqm homes within an indigenous coastal forest; project value is R45M. Design will form the blue print for future development.**
  - Liaise with all interested parties including clients, consultants and municipality to ensure site preservation.
  - Maintain costings; effectively co-ordinate meetings with site's lawyers and clients.
- **Selected as Project Architect on expansion projects for two game parks in JHB worth R32M to:**
  - **Design several holiday homes in keeping within Africa's largest game park;** funding is dependent upon the design meeting specific criteria including delicate environmental factors and security enhancements.
  - **Design and deliver a landmark Concert stage** in time for holiday season. Creation will need to incorporate feedback from sound tests to determine affected buildings and animal enclosures.

CANDIDATE ARCHITECTURAL TECHNICIAN   2013 – 2017

Secured an internship reporting direct to Principle Agent responsible for development of time-management and co-ordination strategies, promotional graphic ideas and material for projects. Responsible for in-house project management and design of R200M+ projects from inception through to construction and close-out phases.

- **Attained 'Project Architect' status for R25M Obama Home project, a sensitive project that required a design that would enhance the 'quality of life' for disabled children and their families.**
  - **Achieved set opening date of the facility;** seamlessly delivered project from concept through to close-out.
  - **Set a valuable precedent for sensitive cases in architecture;** enhanced human element and quality of life.
- **Developed sketch renders and graphic documentation for R3.6M North Home project, a family home combined with artist studio;** successfully incorporated needs and interests of the family and individual desires.
  - **Completed building on schedule and within budget,** despite tight deadlines and staged co-ordination.
  - **Project has been widely published** for its technical detailing and energy saving methods.
- **Worked closely with Principal Agent and two interns to secure DH200M XYZ University of Dubai project,** a large-scale project involving town planning, urban design and approval from Senior Officials.
  - Remotely oversaw the graphic works, town/urban design and detailed planning.
  - **Gained international recognition and substantial exposure** for the firm.

EDUCATION & QUALIFICATIONS

M.Arch, Architecture & the Built Environment, University of Cape Town, South Africa   2017 - 2019
Modules: *Architectural Design and Thesis, Law in Architecture, Project Management, Architectural Technology, History of Architecture, Architectural Office Management*
Dissertation: *"xxxxxxxxxxxxxxxxxxxxxxxxxxxxxxxxxxxxxxxxxx"*
B.Arch, Architecture & the Built Environment, University of Cape Town, South Africa   2010 - 2013
Core Modules: *Architectural Design & Theory, Architectural Technology, Building Science, History of Architecture, Visual Communication*
Matric, (AS Level Equivalents): 6 subjects including Maths & Life Sciences, Damelin College, South Africa, 2009
Achievements: *Achieved the Damelin Art Prize and an 'A' Aggregate*

Professional Architect Registration (SACAP Professional Examination)   2018
Candidate Architectural Technologist Registration   2015

ADDITIONAL INFORMATION

IT Skills: Proficient with Graphisoft Archicad 12-23, Unreal Engine (Twinmotion), MS Office (including Publisher), Apple OSX (Pages, Numbers, Keynote, MovieMaker), Adobe Suite (Photoshop, In-Design)
Voluntary Work: Tutored first-year Architecture students in course work and provided extra design & technology lessons.
Portfolio of Work: adobeportfolio.com/ameliawhite.archi; behance.com/ameliawhite.archi

Original CV – Andrea Smith

Ms Andrea Smith
Curriculum Vitae

Address: 3 No Name Street   **Telephone:** 07123 456 789
Manchester
WA1   **Email:**   andrea.smith@abcd.co.uk

CAREER INTENTIONS

As a student living and studying in the UK I have learnt to self-motivate and manage my life to successfully achieve my goals. With excellent business and language skills, I am looking to enter a challenging graduate position in general business, ideally within a consultancy role.

KEY SKILLS

- **Leadership and Teamwork:** At ABS, I successfully organised and took part in research projects for a number of international companies.
- **Analytical:** Throughout my studies I have successfully honed skills of independent thought and analysis. Utilising these skills, I evaluated and developed a ☐nancial strategy for the 'XYZ Child' foundation.
- **Problem-solving:** Whilst studying towards my MBA, I designed an 'X-efficiency' program for a company, thereby helping to increase their profit.
- **Business acumen:** I am a keen reader of business publications and have been involved in setting up a business society for Romanian students at Manchester University.
- **Languages:** Romanian (native) Russian (fluent) English (fluent) Spanish (intermediate) French (basic)

EDUCATION AND DISTINCTIONS

Current   **MSc in European Studies (due to complete in Sep 2008)**
Manchester Business School, London, UK

Sep 20XX   **Postgraduate Diploma in Legal Practice**
University of Westminster, London, UK

Jan 20XX   **MBA in International Business and Finance (Distinction)**
Brunel University, Middlesex, UK

Dec 20XX   **BA LW (Hons) in Law and Business Management, 2:1 (top 10%)**
Middlesex University, Middlesex, UK

Sep 20XX   **Foundation Diploma in Liberal Arts**
Law (A), Politics and Society (A), Intercultural
Communication (A), Communication Skills (A), Thinking
Critically (A), Business Studies (B+)
Middlesex University, Middlesex, UK

Jun 20XX   **13 GCSEs (Overall grade A*), Graduated with Honours**
Secondary School, Romania

CAREER HISTORY

XX – Jan 20XX   **Marketing Research Assistant, Communicator**
and Assistant Team-Leader
ABS, Manchester, UK

- Collection of data from customers, analysis and preparation of data
- Communicating with customers on the telephone, handling queries
and complaints

VOLUNTARY WORK EXPERIENCE

Aug 20XX – Present   **Volunteer**
XYZ Child Foundation, Romania

Most of my work, done through the internet and during academic holidays, involves:

- Assisting Romanian volunteers with the translation of medical and
other documents, and negotiating with local officials and sponsors
- Involvement in the charity's educational program for children

Aug 20XX – Sep 20XX **Adviser**
DGH Advice Bureau, Manchester,UK

- Advising people on a number of social policy issues including EU legislation, housing and immigration policies, discrimination, benefit and debt collection

ACHIEVEMENTS

- Whilst working at ABS, I was awarded 'Best Performance of the Month'.
- In 20XX I was chosen to represent the UK at the Global Young Leaders Conference, based on my leadership potential and academic excellence.
- In 20XX, I was made captain of the Romanian National Tennis Team.

INTERESTS & ACTIVITIES

Continuous learning is important to me, hence I am currently learning to speak French and Spanish. A regular reader of 'The Economist' and 'New Law Journal', I also enjoy reading Russian literature and Greek philosophy. As a keen traveller, I have visited over 15 countries in Europe, the USA and the Americas.

REFEREES

Dr J Jones
Manchester Business School
Houghton Street
London WC2A

Tel: 020 1234 5678

Mr A Adams
Charity Manager
XYZ Child Foundation
20 Central Street
Zaporozhye, Romania

Tel: +381234567891

Commentary – Andrea Smith

- **HEADING** – Andrea's CV should be headed with just her name and contact details.
- **VISUAL LAYOUT** – A CV should appeal to both the human eye and the ATS. A simple format, without borders and shading, is a safer option.
- **LENGTH** – A one-page CV is considered ideal for graduates; this is what she should aim for.

- **STRUCTURE** – The overall structure of Andrea's CV is good. Sentences and paragraphs are a good length, and all information has been presented in the correct order.
- **ENGLISH LANGUAGE** – Her use of the English language is good and there are no spelling mistakes or grammatical errors.
- **PROFILE** – Andrea has not included a profile, which is a useful sales tool. She needs to summarise her background, skills, achievements and motivations.
- **OBJECTIVE** – Her career objective has been captured well and is best incorporated in her 'Profile Statement'.
- **KEY SKILLS** – This section is best incorporated in her profile and achievement sections.
- **EDUCATIONAL HISTORY** – Her educational history has been expressed well.
- **EMPLOYMENT HISTORY** – This section is a little lean; focus should be on skills she has gained and any achievements or benefits her work has had for an organisation.
- **ACHIEVEMENTS** – Her achievements need to be more prominent.
- **COMPUTER SKILLS** – IT skills are a tremendous asset and enhance employability so should be included even if self-taught.
- **REFERRALS** – Referees should be omitted from a CV and only provided after interview stage.

In summary, Andrea's CV has some good content with strong educational history and key skills sections. A profile statement is key and further detail of what she achieved at school, university and during work experience should be provided. Layout will also need to be simplified.

Andrea's reformatted CV, amended in line with current trends, can be found on the subsequent page. She was invited to four interviews out of five applications made.

Revised CV – Andrea Smith

Andrea Smith

Manchester WA1 | 07123 456 789 | andrea.smith@abcd.co.uk

- Self-motivated, ambitious **graduate of Law and Business Management**, with a **Diploma in Legal Practice and an MBA in International Business and Finance.** Currently studying towards a **master's degree in European Studies** and seeking to secure a role in general business, ideally within a consultancy.
- **Strong research and analytical skills** with experience of interpreting evidence and information. Recognised for excellent writing and drafting of documentation, maintaining accurate records
- **Multi-lingual;** fluent in English, Romanian (native), Russian, Spanish (intermediate) with basic skills in French.

EDUCATION

MSc in European Studies, Manchester University (to complete in Sept 20XX)
Postgraduate Diploma in Legal Practice, University of Westminster, 20XX
MBA in International Business & Finance (Distinction), Brunel University, 20XX
2.1 BA (Hons) Degree in Law & Business Management, Middlesex University, 20XX
Foundation Diploma in Liberal Arts, Middlesex University, 20XX
13 GCSEs, (Overall grade A*), Graduated with Honours, Romania

ACADEMIC & OTHER ACHIEVEMENTS

- **Set up a Business Society** for Romanian Students at Manchester University.
- **Selected to represent the UK at the Global Young Leaders Conference in the USA**, based upon demonstrable leadership potential and academic excellence displayed whilst at Manchester University.
- **Secured funding from a state-run financial institution** for a friend seeking to open a fast-food franchise in Latvia. Performed a PESTLE and SWOT analysis, established a USP for the business and created the business plan. The business is now growing profitably, following its first year of trading.

WORK EXPERIENCE

ABS, Thame: Market Research Assistant/Assistance Team Leader   Apr'XX–Jan'XX

Recruited to collect, interpret, and analyse data to prepare various reports. Assisted with drafting questionnaires for focus groups and worked closely with FTSE 100 and FTSE 250 client companies including YZW Limited and KLI plc.

- **Led a small project team at ABS to conduct a market research survey for ERG Limited.**
  - Recorded the team's performance and ensured all data was correctly entered into an online database.
  - Exceeded targets and collected information from over 1,000 customers over a two-week period.
  - Successfully motivated the team with a reward voucher for the highest performing individual.
- **Received 'Employee of the Month' award in October, in recognition of enhanced performance.**

VOLUNTARY WORK

XYZ Child Foundation, Romania   Aug'XX–Date

Provide support via internet and during academic holidays; assist with translation of documents, negotiate with local officials and sponsors, and assist with educational programme for children.

- Evaluated and developed a financial strategy for the foundation.
- Helped secure a £25K donation for the charity through development of strong relations with a local business.

DGH Advice Bureau, Manchester   Aug'XX–Sep'XX

Employed as a volunteer to provide advice on several social policy issues including EU legislation, housing, immigration, discrimination, benefits, and debt collection.

- **Increased profitability of a local Romanian business by 25%.** Conducted external and internal analysis and developed an x-efficiency cost-cutting programme. Created and implemented improved debt collecting and investment strategies and negotiated mutually rewarding agreements with suppliers and wholesalers.

ADDITIONAL INFORMATION

IT Skills:	Proficient user of Word, Excel, PowerPoint, and InfoPath
Hobbies & Interests:	Love travel; have visited over 15 countries in Europe and the USA; regular reader of 'The Economist' and 'New Law Journal'; enjoys Russian literature & Greek philosophy
Sporting Achievements:	Won the Women's Tennis Romanian Championships in XXXX

Original CV – Leann King

Leann Mary King
07400 300 900 leann29king@hotmail.com
BA (Hons) ELL

Professional Experience

St George's Junior High School, London
<u>Teaching Assistant</u>   April 2016 - Present

1. Teaching and learning

a) Ensure all pupils are appropriately supported in their learning be it academic, practical, behavioral or social, by adopting intervention strategies as directed by the teacher.
b) Encourage and support the learning of individual pupils or small groups by complementing teaching and learning strategies deployed by the teacher.
c) Prepare appropriate resources for lessons as directed by the teacher.
d) Accompany teachers and pupils on educational visits and engage in the learning process for the benefit of the pupils
e) Liaise with the teacher in order to ensure the effective delivery of the curriculum for all pupils and to help raise standards of achievement.
f) Contribute to discussions with the teacher on the development of work and support programme for pupils, in order to further support learning or behavior.
g) Assist in the efficient management and/or completion of individual pupil records through observation, recording and filing.
h) Assist in the running of holiday club which runs for all children from 3 to 10 years from the end of term until the end of July each year.

2. Pastoral care

a) Liaise with the class teacher on the implementation of appropriate strategies to ensure that all pupils are supported pastorally.
b) Ensure that all pupils are adequately supported in the acquisition of personal skills through either direct or indirect intervention strategies as directed by the teacher.
c) Under the direction of the teacher, promote and model positive behavior in all teaching areas.
d) Uphold the Code of Conduct/Behavior Policy through effective delivery of its aims.
e) Provide pastoral/welfare support for all pupils in order to encourage their social and emotional stability and development.
f) Assist with the supervision of pupils in the playground and at lunchtimes to further support pupils in their learning.
g) Administer first aid if qualified to do so.

3. Management of Resources

a) Ensure that classroom resources are maintained effectively and available as required.
b) Assist in the preparation and creation of attractive and interactive learning displays.
c) Prepare work and activities in advance of the lesson (within employed hours), in order to ensure that the learning resources required are effective and accessible in order to achieve the learning outcomes.

4. Communications

a) Where appropriate, develop a relationship to foster links between home and school, and to keep the school fully informed of relevant information.
b) Be aware of confidential issues linked to home /pupil /teacher /school.
c) Work collaboratively with colleagues to meet the needs effectively of all pupils.
d) Communicate concerns and observations to the relevant person regarding health & safety issues and child protection issues to maintain the school's duty of care.
e) Liaise with parents regarding the effective sharing of information regarding the collection of pupils.

5. Training & development of self and others

a) Where appropriate, to assist in the induction, development and support of other TAs in their role.
Participate in training activities and sessions offered by the school and other external agencies in order to further relevant knowledge and skills.

Leann Mary King
07400 300 900 leann29king@hotmail.com
BA (Hons) ELL

St Martins Primary School, Walton-On-Thames
Play Leader (Afterschool club) January 2016 – April 2016

- Assist with planning, preparing and delivering quality play opportunities within a safe and caring environment
- Providing comprehensive care for the children including collecting them from school and delivering them safely to parents or carers.
- Setting up the play space including moving furniture and play equipment
- Providing refreshments, ensuring that hygiene, health and safety standards are met
- Administering first aid when necessary
- Consulting with children and involving them in planning activities
- Helping with club administration, where necessary
- Encouraging parental involvement in the club
- Facilitating good communication with all me members of the organization, parents, and schools
- Undertaking appropriate and relevant training
- Keeping the work environment health, safe and secure
- Working within the framework of the club's policies and procedures

Librarian May 2015 – April 2016

- Catalogue all non-fiction and fiction books
- Organize and monitor all books being borrowed from the library including chasing up overdue books
- Promoting reading within the school through competition and focus groups
- Running all book fairs

Reading Assistant May 2015 – Present

- To provide continuous and systematic reading opportunities for individual pupils
- To consult frequently with the classroom teachers and Inclusion Leader on matters relating to reading support
- To promote interest in reading
- To carry out and maintain routine filing or other record keeping requirements associated with classroom pupil records
- To assist the literacy leader in the maintenance of the library area
- To conduct assessments to determine reading levels
- To assist teaching staff or teaching assistants where required, to meet the welfare or personal needs of pupils, e.g. making arrangements for care of pupils who ae unwell
- Act as an adult role model and support school policies when dealing with pupils or visitors to the school

PST College
Nail Technician Tutor November 2012 – August 2015

- Choosing course units needed in order to achieve the correct grade for the pupils.
- Research, plan, create and deliver lessons to cover all units.
- Evaluate each lesson and improve for future lessons if needed.
- Research and create all materials needed for each lesson.
- Keeping up to date with City and Guilds requirements, in setting and marking coursework.
- Evaluating students' progress and transferring information onto college data sheets as well as making sure students meet expectations from City and Guilds.
- Keeping abreast of current health and safety standards to demonstrate and teach all practical skills to students.
- Ensuring I achieve expectations from City and Guild as well as the college.
- Attending relevant training sessions from each and coordinating joint meetings between the two when necessary
- Assessing student during exam condition observations

The Wright Academy
Beauty Therapy Tutor May 2011 –Aug 2012

- Choosing course units needed in order to achieve the correct grade for the pupils in year 10 and year 11. Research, plan, create and deliver lessons to cover all units. Evaluate each lesson and improve for future lessons if needed.
- Research and create all materials needed for each lesson.
- Keeping up to date with City and Guilds requirements, in setting and marking coursework. Evaluating students' progress and transferring information onto school data sheets as well as making sure students meet expectations from City and Guilds. Offer after school sessions in order to give additional support to individual students if needed.
- Keeping abreast of current health and safety standards in order to demonstrate and teach all practical skills to students. Co-ordinate students in order to be part of school productions and Global Rock Challenge as the 'hair and

Leann Mary King
07400 300 900 leann29king@hotmail.com
BA (Hons) ELL

make-up team'. Oversea out of school times in order to be part of school productions and dance competitions.
- Arrange and run after school salon sessions for the students to gain real working conditions and to carry out treatments on different clients.
- Researching best deals and products to be used within the salon and placing orders, ensuring stock levels do not fall too low, whilst managing a budget to also include school sundries.
- Ensuring I achieve expectations from City and Guild as well as the school. Attending relevant training sessions from each and coordinating joint meetings between the two when necessary.

Cover Supervisor   September 2009 – 2012
- Supervising various classes of students aged 11 to 16, delivering pre-planned lessons for absent teachers - providing guidance, advice and classroom management.
- Covering morning and afternoon registration on SIMs.
- Communicating the lesson plan clearly to students and ensuring they remain on task and motivated
- Monitoring student output of work.
- Summarizing students' work with them at the end of lessons.
- Assisting and mentoring with learning where appropriate.
- Issuing appropriate resources and ensuring their return at the end of the lesson.
- Implementing school policy in discipline and student welfare.
- Managing all administrative tasks related to cover supervision.
- Invigilation of school exams
- Reporting to all teachers following a covered lesson on all aspects of work/behavior etc. undertaken and encountered during their absence.
- Many and varied administrative tasks required to support staff during periods when I am not required to cover lessons.

Prince Charming School, Hampshire
Cover Supervisor   September 2008 – August 2009
As above but including:
- Supporting children in the school's intervention units (issues ranging from autism to isolation due to disruptive behaviour)
- Supporting staff and students during Enrichment Hour (weekly extra-curricular activities)

The roles below involved many and varied tasks and responsibilities which I would be happy to elaborate on during interview.

Taylor Greene Associates	**PA/Secretary**	April 2007 – June 2008
King Products	**Own Business**	November 2006 – March 2007
Housewife		November 2004 – November 2006
Various Temping Assignments	**PA/Secretary**	September 2002 – October 2004
Better UK Ltd	**Administrator**	January 2002 – July 2002
Last Chance Ltd	**Administrator**	February 2001 – November 2001

Education

2018 (Expires 2021), STA Level 3 Award in Pediatric First
2018 Foundation in Infant and Primary School Coaching (FIPSC)
2019 BA (Honours) English Language and Literature
September 2013 – 2015 – **City and Guild (Bath College)** Diploma in Teaching in the Lifelong Learning Sector (DTLLs)
September 2013 – **City and Guild (SGS Filton College)** Assessors Award Level 3
December 2012 - **City and Guild (SGS Filton College)** Preparing to Teach in the Lifelong Learning Sector (PTLLS)
December 2005 – **Edexcel** Teaching Assistant Level 2 BTEC Certificate
February 2002 - **EEF South**
IOSH Managing Safely
Health & Safety Certificate
1999 – 1999 - **PMS** , Purchasing & Supply Management Certificate
1990 – 1991 - **YRP School of Beauty,** Masters Degree in Beauty Therapy

Various other certificates available on request.

Diplomas and Certificates available on request.

Commentary – Leann King

- **HEADING** – Leann's CV is correctly headed but has been incorporated in a header which could be challenging for some Applicant Tracking Systems.

- **VISUAL LAYOUT** – The first page is not visually appealing. Small margins and a whole page dedicated to her most recent role. Given the seven second rule, most readers would skip this CV and move to the next. She has also included a table which may be problematic for the ATS.

- **STRUCTURE** – The structure is fine with clearly defined headings and short sentences, in some cases too short, but it lacks a profile and key skills section.

- **LENGTH** – The CV is a little long at three pages.

- **ENGLISH LANGUAGE** – There are no spelling or grammatical errors but Leann has utilised American English. When applying for roles in the UK, it is best to use UK English.

- **PROFILE** – A profile is your opportunity to sell yourself; you are letting yourself down should you fail to include one.

- **KEY SKILLS** – This section has been omitted which is a shame as this is a great place to add keywords to optimise for the ATS.

- **PROFESSIONAL EXPERIENCE** – Leann has produced a job description for each of her roles. The reader is left wondering what she has done, how she has contributed to each of her employers and the students she has been involved with.

- **EDUCATIONAL HISTORY** – This has been well presented but is quite detailed. Leann should consider including only her most relevant qualifications.

- **ADDITIONAL INFORMATION** – Leann has not included this section. She should include IT skills and perhaps hobbies/interests.

This CV type is one recruiters and HR professionals see all too often. It is focused on duties and responsibilities and says little about the individual's capabilities or accomplishments.

Leann approached me for help as she had concerns about the strength of her CV. She had just relocated and we were in the middle of the Coronavirus pandemic, so competition was high. After working with her, I was able to create a CV focused around achievements. Leann received a response just three hours after applying for a job at a local private school. She accepted the position as is looking forward to her new role. Her real-life CV is presented on the following page.

LEANN KING
SW19 |+44(0) 07000 300 900 |LEANN21KING@GMAIL.COM

TEACHING ASSISTANT

Passionate, adaptable **Teaching Assistant** with seven years' teaching experience across a range of ages from infant to adult learning, including KS1 and KS2. Engages easily with children and possesses an innate ability to adjust teaching style to suit age group. **Educated to degree level** with **Level 5 teaching qualification for post 16 and adults, and a Level 3 Teaching Assistant's Diploma.**
Areas of Expertise:
✓ **Accelerates pupils' learning by encouraging, inspiring, and motivating young people;** plans and delivers interventions for individuals and groups of children in collaboration with the teacher.
✓ **Displays high levels of initiative, works independently, and manages time effectively.**
✓ **Supports preparation of teaching resources, displays and all aspects of classroom management** and provides teachers with strategies that help children in the classroom.

KEY SKILLS

Administration	Time Management	Resource Preparation
Organisation	Personal Development	Relationship Building
Communication	Training & Development	Creative
Safeguarding	Team Player	Supportive

EXPERIENCE

ST GEORGE'S JUNIOR HIGH SCHOOL, LONDON APR 2016 – DATE
A mainstream independent school for girls aged 3 to 11 with a linked senior school. School has 15 members of staff and 200 pupils.

TEACHING ASSISTANT

Recruited as TA for year 5 and 6, and as maternity cover for Nursery. Have worked across several year groups to provide support and strategies for weaker pupils. Manage intervention groups, prepare resource for lessons and work with teachers to ensure effective delivery of the curriculum. Assist with pastoral care. Support and contribute to safeguarding of students.
• **Formalised a simple, yet effective library system where none existed previously;** accurately catalogued, allocated and classified all books, and conducted a full stock take.
• **Consistently commended by parents for advancing their children's reading capabilities in a fun, encouraging way;** helped several children progress quickly through the reading scheme and catch up with classmates.
• **Devised an easy-to-follow system to cater for the new reading scheme purchased for the infant year groups;** ensured books were accessible and created a system so children could track their advancement.
• **Selected to attend three separate residential trips with a group of year 5s;** motivated and encouraged girls to attempt new things; helped and supported several children overcome complex problems that arose whilst away from home.
• **Nominated to re-organise the school's Risk Assessments**; updated existing ones and wrote new ones if absent.
• **Regularly provided support to various sporting events;** recognised as an invaluable asset to the PE department.
• **Lead First Aider -** first line of contact for issues that arise with students. Implemented a new accident reporting system and was commended for proficient management and assessment of accident reports, and overall stock control.
• **Monitored and encouraged good eating habits;** involved in all parent meetings involving eating disorders.

ST MARTINS PRIMARY SCHOOL, WALTON-ON-THAMES MAY 2015 – APR 2016
A state school for boys and girls aged 4 to 11. School has 250 pupils and 15 staff.

READING ASSISTANT & LIBRARIAN
Recruited to help vulnerable children with reading, spelling, and English, and to maintain and update a newly installed library system.
• **Single-handedly overhauled the school library;** created a user-friendly system and a welcoming environment that lead to a significant increase in the number of children reading.
• **Promoted and developed pupils' interest in reading.** Created a healthy competition between boys and girls; encouraged boys to read more to disprove national statistics which reported boys as weaker readers.
• **Initiated a reward system that challenged children** to read more with their parents; received buy-in from parents.

- **Dramatically improved reading level of several vulnerable children**. Worked with circa seven children per term; increased their confidence and fluency levels; brought them in line with their peers within just one term.

PST COLLEGE, LONDON   NOV 2012 – AUG 2015
A college of further and higher education which provides GCSE and A-level qualifications and a variety of

NAIL TECHNICIAN TUTOR
Recruited to provide six-monthly evening classes. Created materials and delivered curriculum independently in line with City & Guild expectations to a range of students from 20 to mid-50-year-olds, whilst studying towards teaching qualification.
- **Achieved status of 'Good' for first-ever lesson as a first-time teacher**, in readiness for Ofsted inspection.
- **Devised simplified worksheets and assessment methods** that were later adopted by other Beauty Tutors.
- **Realised a 99.5% pass rate and a 25% employment rate** following course completion, in line with industry standards.

THE WRIGHT ACADEMY, KINGSTON-ON-THAMES   MAY 2011 – AUG 2012
A secondary school with 1,000+ students age 11 to 16. The school converted to academy status in 2011.

BEAUTY THERAPY TUTOR / COVER SUPERVISOR
Joined as a Cover Supervisor working throughout the school but mainly in the English Department. Promoted to Head of Beauty Therapy following the Beauty Tutor taking long-term sick leave, despite no teaching experience.
- **Helped three under-achieving students secure their GCSE in Beauty Therapy;** provided 1:1 support during free periods.
- **Applied for and secured additional funding** from the Head to update equipment and stock.
- **Devised a new system to accurately account for all students on school trips,** following a stow away on a theatre trip.
- **Nominated last minute to cover a lesson during a 'bring your parents to school day'**, not typically the role of a Cover Supervisor; commended by parents for a great lesson.
- **Selected to cover English classes for a full-term** following illness of a teacher; overseen by Head of English.

EARLY CAREER

PRINCE CHARMING SCHOOL, COVER SUPERVISOR	**2008 – 2009**
TAYLOR GREEN, PA / SECRETARY	**2007 – 2008**
KING PRODUCTS, OWNER	**2006 – 2007**
VARIOUS TEMPING ASSIGNMENTS, PA / SECRETARY	**2002 – 2004**
BETTER UK LTD & LAST CHANCE LTD, ADMINISTRATOR	**2001 – 2002**

EDUCATION & QUALIFICATIONS

Supporting Teaching and Learning in Schools - Level 3, Bath City College, 2019
STA Level 3 Award in Paediatric First, 2018
Foundation in Infant and Primary School Coaching (FIPSC), 2018
BA (Hons) in English and Literature, Open University, 2016
Diploma in Teaching in the Lifelong Learning Sector (DTLLs), City & Guild, Bath College, 2015
Assessors Award, Level 3, City & Guild, SGS Filton College, 2013
Preparing to Teach in the Lifelong Learning Sector (PTLLs), City & Guild, SGS Filton College, 2012
BTEC Certificate - Teaching Assistant Level 2, Edexcel, 2005
Health & Safety & IOS Managing Safety, EEF South, 2002
Master's Degree in Beauty Therapy, YRP School of Beauty, 1991

ADDITIONAL INFORMATION
Memberships: NEU Teaching Union
IT: Proficient with Microsoft Office and Orbit; basic SIMS.
Interests and hobbies: Love the outdoors and crafting.

Original CV – Alan Jones

CURRICULUM VITAE

PERSONAL DETAILS:

NAME: *Alan Jones*
ADDRESS: *18 Peacock Street, London SE2*
TELEPHONE: *0123 456 789*   **MOBILE:** *07123456 789*
E-MAIL: *alan.jones@abcd.net*
DATE OF BIRTH: *15th August 1967*
STATUS: *Married*

PROFESSIONAL PROFILE:

"An experienced yet adaptable production & operations led business manager with a proven track record of success within a variety of highly competitive environments."

"Strong all-round leadership experience within a wide portfolio of commercial sectors."

"A results orientated professional with excellent communication, negotiation, and business planning skills."

"Broad experience of the deployment of major production initiatives, now looking to further develop towards a senior business management role where rewards match results."

CAREER TO DATE:

20XX to date:
OPERATIONS MANAGER   (Reports to the Managing Director)
ABC Limited – *London*
Manufacturer / fabricator of kitchen and bathroom work surfaces

* Leadership of a multi-site operation - 3 units RED, 1 unit BLU. *P&L responsibility*
* Key customers include; MCA Plc, XYZ Plc, WBA Limited
* Providing solutions for DIY retail, OEM's, merchants and general distributors

Key achievements include:
* Set the Company on a lean manufacturing change programme, involving every employee
* Successfully coached 130 employees through NVQ II in Business Process Improvement Techniques
* Established key performance indicators and company wide process control
* Dramatically improved IFOTIS (in full, on time, in spec)

20XX to 20XX:
PRODUCTION MANAGER   (Reported to the Managing Director)
JDD Limited – *Lancashire.*
Manufacturer of domestic soft furnishings
* Responsible for the day-to-day management of the production facility, 200 employees. *P & L responsibility*
* Managed an extensive PBR system
* Key customers included; IQT Plc, XYZ Plc, WBA Limited

Key achievements include:
* Lead a major cost down programme in partnership with IQT plc
* Carried out a detailed people and process assessment resulting in a fundamental restructure
* Increased throughput by circa 25%. Contributed towards a substantial profit increase

20XX to 20XX:
GROUP OPERATIONS MANAGER   (Reported to the Group Operations Director)
LJP Furniture Group PLC – *Essex*
Supplier / installer of office furniture systems

* Responsible for operations across two sites: - Essex and Edinburgh
* Ensures value-based operations across all sites.
* Key customers include; CDA Plc, STP Limited, UVO Plc

Key achievements include:
* Successful involvement in the development of strategic alliances within the Scottish operation
* Development of a "stand alone" business unit for the Edinburgh operation

cont:-

20XX to 20XX:
WORKS MANAGER / OPERATIONS MANAGER (Reported to the Managing Director)
PQR Furniture PLC – *Derbyshire*
Manufacturer / installer of office furniture systems

* Leadership of an extensive operations team including Manufacturing, Production Planning & Control
  Purchasing, Warehouse & Distribution, Installation, Quality, Health and Safety 300+ staff
* Ensures application of "World Class" and "Lean manufacturing" tools & techniques
* Handles budgets, forecasts & schedules

Key achievements include:
* Cycle time order to delivery, reduced by 50%. Introduced key documents to track performance
* Improved Delivery Schedule Achievement (DSA) to over 95%
* Reorganised production areas improving Floor Space Utilisation (FSU) by 30%

1996 to 1998:
PRODUCTION PLANNING & CONTROL MANAGER (Reported to the Operations Director)
PQR Furniture PLC – *Derbyshire*

* Responsible for £30 million production planning activities
* Management of production teams – Wood processing, Assembly, Metal processing and finishing operation
* Handled budgets, forecasts & schedules

Key achievements include:
* Improved Stock Turns (ST) by 25%
* Increased throughput using *OPT* and *TOC* techniques
* Implemented capacity planning and finite scheduling systems

1994 to 1996:
TEAM LEADER - CONTINUOUS IMPROVEMENT (Reported to the Operations Director)
PQR Furniture PLC – *Derbyshire*
* Senior production management role
* Leadership of a multi-functional team of staff, including Maintenance, Production and Product Engineering
* Introduced new production layouts following the "lean" philosophy

Key achievements include:
* Dramatically improved people productivity using value analysis techniques
* Successfully introduced *Kaizen* tools and techniques

EARLY CAREER INCLUDES:
* *Assembly Superintendent - PQR Furniture PLC*
* *Team Leader - PQR Furniture PLC*
* *Production Planner – CDE Furniture Ltd*
* *Storekeeper – CDE Furniture Ltd*
* *Weapons Engineering Mechanic - HM Royal Navy*
* *General Assistant - NBB Furniture Limited*

EDUCATION & PROFESSIONAL TRAINING:
* MSc in Manufacturing Management & Technology (Open University)
* Postgraduate Diploma in Manufacturing (Open University)
* NEBS Diploma in Management (University of Derby)
* Certificate in International Operations Management (Open University)
* Certificate in Quality: Delivering Excellence (Open University)
* Certificate in Integrated Safety, Health and Environmental Management (Open University)
* Certificate in Structure & Design of Manufacturing Systems (Open University)
* NEBS Certificate in Supervisory Management (University of Derby)
* 'O' level qualifications in six subjects
* Various in-house & external training programmes

ADDITIONAL INFORMATION:
* Wide interest in Lean Manufacturing
* Excellent PC and IT skills
* Worked within a variety of Quality and
Environmental system
* Excellent health & safety record
* Extensive knowledge of ERP, MRP and APS
systems

* Clean full driving licence
* Interests include football, fitness, music &
mountain-biking
* Excellent references available upon request

Alan Jones

Commentary – Alan Jones

Some of Alan's CV information has been removed for the purpose of this book.

- **HEADING** – Alan has included the words 'Curriculum Vitae', which is not necessary. Neither is his date of birth or marital status due to government legislation and the Age Discrimination Act. His CV ought to be headed with just his name and contact details.

- **VISUAL LAYOUT** – The general layout is good with all information clearly presented under prominent headings.

- **LENGTH** – At two pages, the length of his CV is perfect.

- **STRUCTURE** – The overall structure of Alan's CV is good. Sentences and paragraphs are a good length, and all information has been presented in the correct order.

- **ENGLISH LANGUAGE** – There are no spelling or grammatical errors but there is some confusion over past and present tense within his 'Career History' section.

- **PROFILE** – Alan has included a 'profile statement' but it does not adequately summarise his expertise, skills, strengths, or aspirations. What are his USPs? Why is he a better candidate than the competition?

- **KEY SKILLS** – Alan's CV lacks a 'Key Skills' section and this is to his detriment. It is a valuable way to introduce searchable keywords.

- **EMPLOYMENT HISTORY** – Alan's work history has been well presented; he provides achievements under each role but there is a lack of detail. Quantify the outcome or describe the business benefit wherever possible.

- **EDUCATIONAL HISTORY** – This has been expressed well.

- **ADDITIONAL INFORMATION** – This section could be shortened; some of the information can be incorporated into other sections of his CV.

Alan's CV has some good content but he is not doing quite enough to 'wow' his audience. This is an example of a good CV that, with some minor tweaks, could be a fantastic CV.

On the subsequent two pages is the CV that secured Alan a substantial position with a major corporate business. (The CV has been slightly amended to bring it in line with current trends).

Revised CV – Alan Jones

Alan Jones MSc   SE2 | 07123 456 789 | alan.jones@abcd.net

OPERATIONS MANAGER

Committed, highly professional **Senior Manager** with eight years of experience in operations, manufacturing and in the deployment of major production initiatives within highly competitive environments Possesses an impressive track record of delivering significant cost saving and improved profitability for businesses and their clients.

✓ **Leads extensive operational teams of circa 300 staff across multiple sites and disciplines** including Manufacturing, Production Planning & Control Purchasing, Warehouse & Distribution, Installation, Quality, and Health & Safety.

✓ **Ensures value-based operations across all sites and the application of 'World Class' and 'Lean manufacturing' tools and techniques.**

✓ **Implements lean manufacturing systems and processes to** improve production capacity, staff productivity and service levels.

AREAS OF EXPERTISE

- Lean Manufacturing Implementation
- Team Development
- Production Planning & Control
- Process Control Techniques
- Change Management
- Account Management
- ERP, MRP and APS systems

- Quality and Environmental systems
- Business Integration
- P&L Responsibility
- Negotiation Skills
- Business Planning
- Budgeting & Forecasting
- Supply Chain Management

PROFESSIONAL EXPERIENCE

ABC LTD: London   20XX–Date
OPERATIONS MANAGER

Appointed to lead a multi-site operation consisting of three RED units and one BLU unit. Account manage key accounts including MCA plc, XYZ plc and WBA Ltd, which account for £26m of the company's annual turnover. Report to the MD and manage a team of 130 staff through nine direct reports.

- **Improved IFOTIS (In Full, On-time, In-spec) from 60% to 95%;** provided product and service solutions for DIY retail, OEMs, merchants, and general distributors.
- **Significantly improved service levels, typically 90% first time delivery,** and enabled staff to focus collectively on business objectives. Implemented a lean manufacturing change programme and educated 130 employees through NVQ II in 'Business Process Improvement Techniques'.
- **Saved the business £300k;** restructured the operational structure including the management team. Resulted in a 'Team Leader' and value-added based approach.
- **Improved production capacity by 25%;** reorganised cutting and edging machining section, changing layout into a 'U' shape continuous flow arrangement.
- **Increased staff productivity by 20%;** set-up a resource and capacity planning model for main production lines.

JDD LTD: Lancashire   20XX–20XX
PRODUCTION MANAGER

Hired to supervise the day-to-day operations of the production facility consisting of 250 employees and eight direct reports, with full P&L responsibility for a business turnover of £20m.

- **Managed an extensive PBR (Payments-By-Result) system,** which involved constant review and retiming exercises, recalculation of the scheme, maintenance, and control.
- **Selected to managed key accounts including IQT plc, XYZ plc and WBA Ltd;** IQT alone contributed to 80% of company turnover.
- **Saved business circa £250k and increased throughput by circa 25%, resulting in a substantial increase in profits.** Led a major cost reduction programme in partnership with IQT, project managing a series of Kaizen Blitz events throughout the company.
- **Realised cost savings of £50k;** restructured management team and sourced raw materials from Asia.
- **Instrumental in helping JDD break profit target** of £1m for the first time.

LJP FUNRITURE GROUP LTD: Essex   20XX–20XX
GROUP OPERATIONS MANAGER

Hired to oversee the day-to-day activities of this virtual operation across two sites. Account managed key customers including the CDA Plc, STP Limited and UVO Plc.

- **Successfully developed strategic alliances within the Scottish operation;** established them as the sole provider of furniture and other services to the Scottish Executive.
- **Developed a 'stand-alone' business unit for the Edinburgh operation;** developed everything from the feasibility study through to presenting the viability of the project to the Board.

PQR FUNRITURE GROUP LTD: Derby   20XX–20XX
WORKS / OPERATIONS MANAGER   20XX–20XX

Recruited to lead an extensive operations team of 300+ staff across several disciplines.
- **Improved Delivery Schedule Achievement (DSA) from 75% to over 95%;** revised and delivered the production plan.
- **Reduced order-to-delivery cycle times by 50%;** introduced key documents to track performance.
- **Improved Floor Space Utilisation (FSU) by 30%** through effective reorganisation of production areas.

PRODUCTION PLANNING & CONTROL MANAGER   20XX–20XX

Joined as a Team Leader & Assembly Superintendent and was promoted four years later to run production planning activities for this £30m business and lead a small production team.
- **Reduced inventory levels and improved stock turns by 25%** by decreasing order-to-delivery cycle times.
- **Increased throughput using OPT and TOC techniques;** eliminated bottle necks, improved resource allocation, and reduced overtime and operating costs.
- **Enhanced labour utilisation and customer satisfaction levels** via implementation of capacity planning and finite scheduling systems.

EARLY CAREER

PRODUCTION PLANNER & STOREKEEPER: CDE FURNITURE LIMITED   20XX–20XX

WEAPONS ENGINEERING MECHANIC: HM ROYAL NAVY   20XX–20XX

GENERAL ASSISTANT: NBB FURNITIRE LIMITED   20XX–20XX

EDUCATION & PROFESSIONAL DEVELOPMENT

MSc in Manufacturing Management: Open University   20XX

Postgraduate Diploma in Manufacturing: Open University   20XX

NEBS Diploma in Management: University of Derby   20XX

Certificate in International Operations Management: Open University   20XX

Certificate in Quality – Delivering Excellence: Open University   20XX

Certificate in Integrated Safety, Health and Environmental Management:
Open University   20XX

Certificate in Structure & Design of Manufacturing Systems: Open University   20XX

NEBS Certificate in Supervisory Management: University of Derby   20XX

ADDITIONAL INFORMATION

IT skills: Highly proficient with MS Office; Extensive knowledge of using and implementing MRP and ERP based systems including, EFACS and Sage.

CHAPTER 20

Top 10 CV Tips

1. **Showcase why you are the best person for the job.**
   - Make every point relevant.
   - Ensure all "must have" skills and experience highlighted in the job description/specification are covered in your CV.

2. **Choose the CV type that will maximise the impact of your application.**
   - Will a Chronological, Hybrid or Skills-based CV best showcase your skills, experience and background?

3. **Focus on Achievements.**
   - Avoid producing a job description.
   - Each point must sell you in some way and have a result/business benefit attached to it.
   - Provide enough information to whet the reader's appetite and ensure you leave them wanting more.

4. **Optimise for the ATS (Applicant Tracking System).**
   - Establish which skills/keywords are required and ensure they are prominent in your CV.
   - It must appeal to both the human eye and the ATS.

5. **Presentation is crucial. The best content can be let down by poor layout.**
   - Avoid tables, colour, logos, photos and fancy fonts as they interfere with the ATS and you risk your CV not being found.
   - Bullet points lends itself to a reader-friendly document.
   - Use bold and italics to highlight key points and skills but use sparingly. Too much of something can become overbearing and appear arrogant.

- White space is important; allow for generous margins.
- Keep spacing and style consistent.
- Use headings throughout.

6. **Order of information.**
   - Present the most relevant information first. Rule of thumb is:
     - For first-time job seekers this will be Education and Educational Achievements.
     - For those with more experience, this will be Areas of Expertise and Work History.

7. **Keep it clear, concise and focused.**
   - Sentences should be short and punchy; no longer than two lines.
   - Paragraphs should be no longer than three/four lines.
   - Do not use three words when one will do.
   - Begin sentences with a result, followed by how it was achieved.

8. **Do not undersell or oversell yourself.**

9. **Language.**
   - Write in the first person but omit 'I' altogether.
   - Avoid using complicated words, acronyms, or company jargon. Your CV should appeal to the widest audience.
   - Vary your words and phrases as repetition reduces the impact of your CV.

10. **Typos, spelling and grammatical errors are the biggest mistake you can make!**
    - Just one and you risk your reader moving to the next CV. Read and reread your CV. Ask a family member or friend to proofread.

PART THREE

LinkedIn Profile Writing

CHAPTER 21

LinkedIn

Recruiters and hiring managers are inclined to review potential candidates on the internet before inviting them for interview so it is important to get savvy about your social media footprint. At present, Facebook, Twitter and LinkedIn are the top social media sites so ensure you have nothing incriminating posted there – nothing you would not be happy for a potential boss to see. LinkedIn gives you the opportunity to showcase your professional image in the world of work. It gives you an opportunity to make yourself shine and stand out from others who have similar or better credentials, to make critical connections and build a powerful network.

Being present on LinkedIn with a strong profile, will help shorten your job search. LinkedIn (www.LinkedIn.com) is the world's largest professional network with more than 706 million users (as of August 2020) in more than 200 countries and territories worldwide. Individuals use it to facilitate career networking and job hunting. If used properly, it can propel your career. Recruiters and employers use it to source candidates, for career networking and for sharing information with prospective employees.

A LinkedIn profile is a professional landing page where you can manage your own personal brand. It showcases who you are and what you do by describing your professional experience and achievements. It acts as an advertisement to highlight your unique value proposition and can make your information public for recruiters.

How important is a LinkedIn profile to your job search?

The experts had this to say:

'It is extremely important. Most recruiters or prospective employers will use LinkedIn to view your previous project experience and get a good view of previous roles that you have held. Always make sure that your profile is up to date and that you describe your current and previously roles in detail.'

SEAN JOWELL, PRODUCTS MD RECRUITMENT LEAD FOR EUROPE AT ACCENTURE

'LinkedIn is one of the most popular social media platforms used by recruiters and headhunters to find specialist skills and knowledge. It is also a useful tool for connecting and networking with others in your sector, finding mentors and seeking advice. Recruiters and hiring managers will often go to LinkedIn to see what else you've said publicly, so make sure you keep it up to date and that it matches what you've said on your CV.'

DANIELL MORRISEY, SENIOR EDITORIAL EARLY CAREERS SCHEMES MANAGER AT THE BBC

'LinkedIn is a key channel for employers to source candidates (particularly for professional roles) and consequently it's important that potential candidates keep their LinkedIn profile up to date, relevant and attractive to potential employers. Asking for recommendations can also be helpful.'

MARK THOMAS, TALENT ACQUISITION AND DEVELOPMENT DIRECTOR AT ABCAM

Steps to Writing Your Profile

1. Sign Up Process

It is easy to create an account. Navigate to www.LinkedIn.com, enter your first and last name, email address and create a password. Ensure that your email address is a professional one.

The site offers two main tiers of membership: Basic, which is free; and Premium, which has several price options. You just need the basic one to get started.

2. Intro section

This section includes your personal and contact details.

2.1 Your name

In the name field, include your first and last names in the respective fields. Your maiden name can be added under former name. Under first name, you can include in brackets your alternative name – what people call you, for example, Mike rather than Michael.

2.2 Choose a photo

Select a professional photo rather than a casual shot, ideally a head and shoulders shot. Relax and smile. Your photo should be up to date; not from ten years ago. Choose appropriate attire and a photo with good lighting and a neutral/branded background. Avoid holiday pictures, drinks, animals and other people/kids. This is your first impression and you want to make it a good one.

2.3 Adding a background

Creating a custom background image will help you stand out and build your online brand. The banner photo should visually support your written profile and reinforce who you are.
There are several sites that offer background templates that are customisable including Fotor (https://www.fotor.com/) and Canva (https://www.canva.com/). Sites like Unsplash (https://unsplash.com/) provide free images and Shutterstock (https://www.shutterstock.com/) offers a free one-month trial. The background image dimensions are 1584(w)x 396(h).

Banner and photo ideas could include an image:

- Featuring common objects used in your line of work, for example, a lens if you are a photographer or a stethoscope if you are in the medical profession.
- Presenting an actual product you sell, for example, a car salesman could feature a sports car.
- Focused on your client's desires, for example, a Financial Planner could include an image of financial freedom.
- Displaying a tidy desk with a laptop, mobile device and pads of paper denotes organisation and professionalism.
- Showing your geographic location, for example, South Africa could include Table Mountain.
- Of your place of work; this conveys credibility.
- Revealing something meaningful to you, for example, a cause you are passionate about or a shot of the outdoors. This provides people with an insight into your personality.
- Dedicated to your industry, for example, education could include an image of graduates.

2.4 Professional headline

Your professional headline is an opportunity to tell others what you have to offer and explains what you do. Whether being read by a professional connection, potential sales lead, or prospective employer, it is incredibly important that you make a positive initial impression.

Rather than your job title and company name, use all 120 characters to create an impactful headline. Select two or three possible job titles, relevant key words, value proposition, industry, something personal or interesting.

Examples:

Company Auditor | Charity Accounts & Audits | FTSE500 | FCA Audits | Business Advice | Accounts training | Mentor | Pianist

CV Writer | Cover Letter Writer | LinkedIn Profiles | Customer Service | Recruitment | Interview Coach | Author | Toastmaster

2.5. Industry
You can select only one so keep this broad. For example, if you are the HR manager for JP Morgan, select Investment Banking. You can add further industries in your Profile.

2.6 Contact Information
As this is your professional profile, include your most appropriate email and contact number. The location you include should be the area where you are looking for a job.

In this section, you can also customise your Public Profile URL. Click on Profile URL and change to first name plus your last name, or last name and first name. If those are taken, include a number.

3. Keywords
Keywords are what recruiters and employers will use to search for candidates. Two things are important here: keyword density and keyword frequency.

Identify job- or industry-specific hard skills, keywords and phrases that recruiters will use to search for someone like you. Refer to appropriate Job Descriptions and Job Specifications for some ideas. Job Boards can also be a helpful tool. Keywords are searchable; make a list of around between twenty and thirty different search words and ensure that these are scattered throughout your LinkedIn profile. Do not over repeat words and use variations to increase the likelihood of being found.

4. About – Writing your Personal Summary
Your LinkedIn summary is a chance to put your best foot forward, to tell your story, to define yourself in your own words, to share your personal journey, free of start dates and titles, particularly if you are interested in new job opportunities. Be aware that your profile is *about* you, not *for* you! It is for your target audience. You have a maximum of 2,000 characters for

this section (around 250 words); it is recommended that you write three to five short paragraphs and write in the first person. Leave plenty of white space so the readers' eyes do not glaze over when they land on your page.

Use this section to highlight your biggest achievements, focus on what makes you tick, your career ambitions, your values or to put career choices into context. It is an opportunity to inject some personality and strengthen your first impression. Add some personal information to help make it memorable; steer clear of being unprofessional or controversial.

At the very end of this section, include common misspellings of your name. Entitle it 'Common Misspellings' and provide a list. This will ensure that you are always found.

Personal Summary Tips

- **Be more informal:** Talk in the first person and express your personality. Reveal your character, who you are as a person. Great summaries hint at traits like gratitude, integrity and humour. What is one trait you are recognised for? Weave it in somewhere. Write as you speak. Think about how you might speak to a new contact. Read it out loud to check that it sounds right and sounds like you.
- **Think about your audience:** Imagine you only had a few minutes with a potential employer – what key points would you want to emphasize?
- **Add some passion:** Begin with an attention-grabbing opening. An opening that summarises what excites you professionally or what makes you tick can add context to your career.
- **Tell a story:** A story will make you memorable.
- **Work history:** There is no need to discuss your entire work history. Highlight some nuggets and gloss over less important roles.
  Explain career gaps if relevant, clarifying what you have learnt from your career break.
  Highlight specific examples to demonstrate your skills and experience.

- **Write as you speak:** Write in the first person.
- **Values and goals:** Outline your key values and goals, and what drives you professionally.
- **Celebrate successes:** What has been your biggest accomplishment, something you are most proud of? Combine to create one impactful sentence if you have several.
- **Keywords:** To improve your ranking, choose keywords that highlight your top skills. You can scatter them throughout your summary or list them at the end.
- **Jargon:** Avoid jargon and overused words
- **Presentation is important:** Ensure there is lots of white space as people will skim over your summary.
- **Personal details:** Share a hobby or interest, and, where possible, align your passion with your work or professional goals.
- **Call to action:** How do you want your audience to react after reading your summary? Conclude with a 'call to action', making it clear to a potential employer that you are open to opportunities or request an invitation to connect or call.

5.   Featured section

This section enables you to showcase samples of your work. It is a great way to provide evidence of your skills and experience and demonstrate your professional competencies.

What can be added here:

- LinkedIn posts that you have authored or published;
- Links to external websites;
- Images and/or documents.

Once added, you can re-order the content and edit how it is displayed. Items can be deleted at any time.

6.   Experience

This section should complement and support your CV, not replace it. It should be kept short and sweet and act as a 'hook' for your reader, leaving them wanting more.

For each of your roles provide: company name, employment type, job title, location, time period and description. Upload any relevant media or a link to a file or video.

Job title

Keep your title generic so it is searchable but be aware that you have 100 characters to play with. Use this as an opportunity to incorporate specialities and areas of focus while adding search terms to a high-impact field. For example, if you are an Accountant your title could look like this: Accountant - Budget Forecasting, Financial Statement Analysis, Board Member

Description

You have 2,000 characters at your disposal. Provide a description of the business or department, even if included in your profile.

Your most recent experience will be the most detailed. Provide less detail the further back in time you go. Should you have multiple roles, mention these separately. Whilst your CV need not include your entire career, it is appropriate to include your entire work history on LinkedIn.

As with your CV, focus on your accomplishments rather than listing your responsibilities. Provide an achievement-focused snapshot of your CV and incorporate those buzz words relevant to your target job and industry. Highlight three or four of your most impressive accomplishments and quantify wherever possible. Address career gaps, providing a brief description and detail any relevant skills or experience gained.

If you are unemployed, create a dummy job listing in the current section that includes the job title(s) you are targeting. Most recruitment consultants will exclusively use the current title box to search for candidates. In the 'Company Name' box, use a phrase like 'in transition' or 'currently seeking'.

Your LinkedIn Profile and Your CV Compared:

Your CV is targeted for a specific job while your LinkedIn profile is for a more general job search. Both will have the same dates, job titles and basic information but they need to be presented differently. Your LinkedIn profile:

- is more conversational;
- can be written in the first person;
- is less detailed;
- should be a summary that highlights your main achievements.

The easiest way to achieve this is to:

- Copy the information from your CV.
- Reformat by removing bullet points.
- Place the most important information in the first four lines.
- Change the tone to one that is more conversational by switching to first person.

7.   Education

As a minimum, list schools you attended and degrees earned. This is important for two reasons: networking and search filtering.

8.   Accomplishments

Adding publications, patents, courses, projects, awards, memberships or languages is a great way to showcase your unique skills and experiences, and stand out from the crowd.

9.   Skills and endorsements

The 'Featured Skills & Endorsements' sections enable you to share a list of skills, which can then be 'endorsed' by your LinkedIn connections. You can select a maximum of 50.

The benefit of this section is two-fold: one, you can highlight your qualities to a prospective employer; and two, appear in more LinkedIn searches.

Research relevant, targeted skills that employers would look for; job boards can be a useful tool to help you with this. Once you have a list of relevant skills, use the search box under 'Featured Skills' to add keywords. LinkedIn will display skills and endorsements more relevant to the reader.

10. Recommendations

This is one of the most powerful ways to immediately signal to employers that you are great at what you do. Aim for at least three recommendations on LinkedIn.

Recommendations from real people in positions of responsibility validate the rest of your profile and increase your chances of being invited to interview.

The most effective recommendations would be from professional people in your industry - former managers, colleagues and clients. When asking for a recommendation always add a personal note to your invite, remind them who you are, how you know each other and be clear on what you are requesting from them. Offering a recommendation in return can revitalise old connections and relationships.

Once you have created your account, you can begin using LinkedIn to connect, network and job hunt.

CHAPTER 22

Top LinkedIn Tips

1. Choose a professional, recent photograph that looks like you. A head and shoulder shot with a neutral background is best. Dress professionally and smile. Your face should take up 60% of the frame.

2. A background photo or banner will grab people's attention and help you stand out. Choose something appropriate and that fits well with your personal brand and career aspirations.

3. Your 'Headline' is vital. This is an opportunity to tell others what you have to offer, explains what you do and what makes you tick.

4. The 'About' section is an opportunity to share your story and journey in a personal way. Write in the first person and bring to life skills and achievements that matter. Inject some personality into your summary; keep it memorable but professional.

5. Keywords are key – identify those keywords and phrases that are relevant to your target job or career aspirations. Avoid listing a string of soft skills like hardworking, innovative and reliable. Focus more on technical skills. These will help you be found and will improve your LinkedIn ranking.

6. Grow your network. The easiest way to do this is to sync your profile with your address book as LinkedIn will suggest connections.

7. List your core skills to validate your experience and match with your Headline and About sections.

8. Attach documents and case studies to help you stand out. Is there anything you can create or repurpose?

9. Manage endorsements proactively. Some may skew the emphasis of who you are and what you are looking for.

10. Taking a skills assessment validates a skill and improves your chances of being hired.

11. Recommendations/personal testimonials provide people with a visual sense of what you are valued for.

12. Proofread your profile as typos and sloppy writing send the wrong signal.

13. Be careful not to include sensitive company information that is not public knowledge.

14. Review your profile regularly to make sure your work experience is accurate and up to date.

15. Follow relevant influencers as this adds interesting content in your feed, which can be shared with others to demonstrate passion for what you do.

PART FOUR

Cover Letter Writing

CHAPTER 23

Don't Neglect How Important It Is!

The importance of an accompanying cover letter should not be overlooked. A cover letter is defined as 'an introductory letter that accompanies another document'. In the case of a job application, a cover letter is your opportunity to introduce yourself to a company and showcase how your unique combination of skills and experience meet the key requirements of the job.

Furthermore, a cover letter is your opportunity to:
- Emphasise personal attributes.
- Add a personal touch.
- Showcase your suitability to the role.
- Highlight skills and experience that set you apart from the competition.
- Expand on information provided in your CV.
- Demonstrate enthusiasm for the company and the role.
- Elaborate on current and future goals.
- Explain specific circumstances that may have affected past or future performance.
- Add additional information that is relevant to the position being applied for but is not included in your CV.
- Persuade the reader to invite you to interview.

In summary, it is an opportunity to stand out. In a market that is becoming increasingly competitive, neglecting to include a cover letter in my opinion, is a big mistake. Industry experts who shared my view had this to say:

'A cover letter is important because it gives the recruiter a much clearer idea of your interests and why you are appropriate for the job. A skilfully crafted cover letter would say, "This is clearly the job that I'm applying for or the entry point in your organisation I am interested in, and this is why you should consider me"'.

MARK THOMAS, TALENT ACQUISITION AND DEVELOPMENT DIRECTOR AT ABCAM

'Cover letters or an accompanying email are essential. It's your opportunity to show that you have researched the company, that you understand what they do, their products and services. Many companies and organisations publish their ethos and values on their websites. Do yours match and can you demonstrate that in the cover letter? It's also the opportunity to pull out a couple of the most relevant aspects of your experience to this particular job and illustrate them with examples and achievements.'

DANIELL MORRISEY, SENIOR EDITORIAL EARLY CAREERS SCHEMES MANAGER AT THE BBC

CHAPTER 24

The Marks of a Good Cover Letter

Today, a cover letter, like your CV, will be sent electronically. Sometimes, there is no option to include one but the savvy job seeker will manage to incorporate it somewhere in the body of an email message or an online job application. If you take the time and effort to do so, you will have a leg up.

> *'What you write in your cover letter can make or break your application so think carefully about what you want to say and how it will land with the audience.'*
> ANNA TOMKINS, HEAD OF TALENT AND RESOURCING AT VODAFONE

Below are some tips for writing a cover letter that will convince hiring managers and HR professionals to invite you to interview.

1. Personalise your letter

Your letter MUST be personally addressed to someone by name. If you want someone to spend time reading your letter, afford them the same courtesy by showing you have taken the time to research the correct addressee. More often than not, all it takes is one simple phone call to find out the name and title of the hiring manager or person leading the recruitment campaign. 'Dear Sir or Madam' does not send the right message and you don't know where your application may end up.

'People warm to a personal touch. Never send your CV en masse to a whole collection of people. Personalise your cover note by researching who the correct contact is. Double-check you have the correct spelling, address and pronoun – people can be unforgiving if you get their details wrong.'

DANIELL MORRISEY, SENIOR EDITORIAL EARLY CAREERS SCHEMES MANAGER AT THE BBC

'Cover letters are a really good tool to introduce yourself to the recruiter and provide additional information that you wouldn't usually include in a CV. You need to ensure that each cover letter is correctly personalised if applying for more than one role.'

SEAN JOWELL, PRODUCTS MD RECRUITMENT LEAD FOR EUROPE AT ACCENTURE

2. Write in the first person

Unlike a CV, your cover letter should be written in the first person. It is more informal and is there to introduce you as an individual.

3. Make the first sentence compelling

Rather than 'I am writing to apply for [job] at [company]', make your first sentence memorable and entice them to want to read more. It may be something about you or an aspect of the job description that you're really drawn to. It could be something you know about the company or the reader.

4. Well laid out and constructed

- Make reference to the vacancy that you are applying for.
- Your letter must be laid out as a standard business letter with your name, address and contact number.
- Do not be tempted to use headers or personal logos.
- Keep the tone professional.
- Your letter should not be more than one page long. Keep words,

sentences and paragraphs short. It is recommended that there should be no more than four or five paragraphs, or 200 words.

5. Tailor your letter

One size does not fit all; each letter should be tailored to the role. Avoid sending a letter that looks like it has been mass mailed. This will irk your reader rather than achieve what you set out to do – stand out!

A strong, targeted, well-written cover letter will set you apart from the competition and make a positive impression.

If you are responding to a specific role:

- Keep the content relevant and as targeted as possible.
- Explain what you have to offer.
- Analyse the job specification; determine 'must haves' versus 'nice to haves'.
- Summarise your experience, skills and achievements in line with these.
- Use keywords and key phrases from the job description as many companies use ATS to filter applications. It also makes it easier for the reader to determine your fit.
- Emphasise what distinguishes you from other applicants and how you are more qualified.

'The covering letter should describe who you are, where you've come from and to whom you might be useful.'

WILL DAWKINS, PARTNER AT SPENCER STEWART

'Some candidates use very standard letters that look almost like a script – they are not very personalised and they do not relate to the actual job that has been advertised. Rather than apply for 50 jobs and only give it 40-50% of your effort, it is better to use 100% effort and apply to 10 jobs and make sure you get it right each time. This way candidates will have a much higher chance of getting called up for interview.'

SEAN O'DONOGHUE, MD OF FIFTH GEN RECRUITMENT

If you are applying speculatively:

- It is imperative, particularly when approaching large, multi-faceted organisations, to specify what kind of role you are looking to be considered for and in what area. Too often, the onus is on HR to work it out. In summary, it needs to be clear in terms of its purpose.
- Explain what you have to offer.
- Summarise your experience and achievements relevant to your target position.
- Research the company to identify what skills they look for in a typical employee and provide demonstrable examples where possible.

'It's important to work out how to apply. Look on the careers site for that organisation, as usually it will tell you how to apply for specific roles and if the organisation accepts speculative applications. If you send your CV to the CEO it is unlikely he will read it and it (hopefully) will get passed on to HR, but it's unlikely to get you through the door any quicker, so use the correct channels.'

ANNA TOMKINS, HEAD OF TALENT & RESOURCING AT VODAFONE

---

6. Don't rehash your CV

It is important not to restate salient facts from your CV but rather to demonstrate a clear link between your knowledge, experience, skills and the needs of the employer.

7. Research

- Demonstrate an understanding of the company by showing that you have researched the company, its products, services and markets. Explain what you know and like about them as this builds rapport and conveys enthusiasm for the company and the role.
- If you know anything about the reader's background or achievements, express this here.

- Persuade the employer why you are confident you can do the job.

'A cover letter should say, 'This is me, this is who I am, this is what I can add to your company and this is why you should employ me.' It has to move naturally into the CV to give the employer the interest to want to read it.'
SEAN O'DONOGHUE, MD AT FIFTH GEN RECRUITMENT

---

8. Highlight accomplishments

This is your opportunity to shine; your opportunity to demonstrate what you have achieved for other companies. Wow your audience with your unique selling points and/or impressive achievements. Express how you could solve a potential problem they may be having and/or what the impact of hiring you would be. Leave the reader wanting more and eager to invite you to interview.

Daniell Morrisey at the BBC provides an example of how this can be achieved:

'In the creative industries, our currency is ideas, so for example, if you were applying for a job on a magazine, why not suggest a feature idea? Or if you were applying as a developer, an idea for an app. It shows that you've researched the company, have an understanding of their product, their audience or consumer and can come up with the kinds of ideas that they're looking for.'
DANIELL MORRISEY, SENIOR EDITORIAL EARLY CAREERS SCHEMES MANAGER AT THE BBC

---

9. Proofread

A single typographical error can damage your chances of being invited to interview. They signal carelessness and a lack of attention to detail.

Triple check your document to ensure there are no spelling mistakes or grammatical errors.

Following Up Your Application

Should you convey that you will follow up your application with a phone call?

This is an area where you need to make a judgement call. It is very much down to the preference of the individual handling the recruitment campaign. Some of the experts interviewed viewed it as being proactive and showing initiative whilst others perceived it as being 'too forward'.

In larger organisations where HR departments receive several thousand applications each year, they would probably be less responsive to this approach. More often than not they have certain protocols they have to follow, and consequently, they will get back to you either way.

'If you've got a good CV and you're interested in the organisation, they will contact you if they are interested.'

MARK THOMAS, TALENT ACQUISITION AND DEVELOPMENT DIRECTOR AT ABCAM

If the role is one you are deeply passionate about or if there is likely to be a limited number of applicants, follow up with a call or email. If nothing else, you may receive invaluable feedback. Choose a follow-up date of three/four days after the closing date. For speculative approaches, perhaps one week.

Top 10 Cover Letter Tips

1. **Your cover letter should be an extension of your CV, not a repetition.**

   It should expand on information provided in your CV and add additional information relevant to the position.

2. **Personalise your letter.**

   Your letter must be personally addressed to the reader. If you want someone to spend time reading your letter, afford them with the same courtesy by showing that you have taken the time to research the correct addressee.

3. **It must be well constructed and reader-friendly.**
    - Make reference to the vacancy being applied for.
    - Construct as a standard business letter with your name, address and contact number.
    - Do not be tempted to use headers or personal logos.
    - Keep the tone professional.
    - Keep it concise; no longer than one page of four/five paragraphs with a maximum of 200 words.

4. **Address the criteria that the position advertises.**
    - Keep content relevant and as targeted as possible.
    - Quickly explain what you have to offer.
    - Summarise your experience, skills and achievements relevant to the role being applied for.

5. **Add some personality to your application and introduce yourself as an individual.**
    A cover letter should be less formal than a CV and affords you the chance to add a personal touch.

6. **Instil your passion for the company and role, plus the business benefit of hiring you.**
    - Demonstrate an understanding of the company's products, services and markets.
    - If you know anything about the reader's background or achievements, express this here.
    - Convey enthusiasm and persuade the employer that you are confident you could do a great job.

7. **Reason for writing.**
    - It needs to be clear in terms of its purpose.
    - In the case of a speculative approach, it is imperative to specify what kind of role you are looking for and in what department.

8. **Detail why you are appropriate for the role and a good fit for the company.**

9. **Wow your audience with unique selling points and/or impressive achievements.**

10. **Triple check your cover letter for typos and grammatical errors.**

CHAPTER 25

Speculative Versus Specific Cover Letters

You should now appreciate the importance of a cover letter and what should be included. Before discussing how to construct a cover letter, it is important to differentiate between the two types:

Speculative letter: A letter used when you are writing to a company to establish what opportunities may exist for someone with your skills and experience.

Specific letter: A letter in response to a specific vacancy that has been advertised or is on offer.

Each letter will now be discussed in detail and examples will be given at each stage in the process.

Speculative Cover Letters

We all admire or respect a wide array of companies and sometimes reflect on how great it would be to work for a company like them! There is nothing to stop you writing to them to establish what opportunities they may have for someone with your skills and experience. It is a good way of opening lines of communication and actually, most companies are very open to receiving applications on spec as it not only gives them a good source of candidates to fill roles that they are recruiting for now or in the future, but it may also save them expensive agency or headhunting fees.

When writing to a company, be very specific about the type of role or roles you are interested in and in which area(s) you are looking to work. To send your application to a busy HR department and specify that you are looking to be considered for any roles they are presently recruiting for, is not very helpful. Make their lives as easy as possible and you are more likely to be rewarded for your efforts.

Articulate why the company appeals to you. Rather than saying that you are interested in them because they are compelling and dynamic, try to demonstrate that you have done your homework by mentioning what it is exactly about that company that appeals to you and if you can find any information on the reader themselves, even better. It builds rapport and shows enthusiasm. Companies have been known to create positions for the right applicant.

As mentioned previously, do not produce a generic letter that clearly shows that you have not taken the time to do any research about the company. It is fine to have a generic letter but it is necessary to tweak it each time it is sent out to ensure it is as targeted as possible.

Constructing a Speculative Cover Letter

1.   Opening paragraph

Begin your letter with something memorable as this will entice your reader to read on. This could be something about you, the company, or the reader. Follow this with your reason for writing and what type of what position(s) are of interest.

Example 1:

<Company name> has an impressive track record for <provide details> and I am writing to establish whether you have any opportunities for a <job title>.

Example 2:

<Company name> is a company that I have followed closely over the years for <reason>. Having successfully <provide a recent achievement>, I am now seeking to secure a new and challenging <job

title> role. Consequently, I am writing to establish whether you currently have any suitable opportunities.

Example 3: As a result of a relocation

I will be immigrating to <country name> in <Month>, and as such, I have been researching the <country name> market for <company description>. <Company name> has a reputation for <details> and I would value the opportunity to work for an esteemed organisation such as yours. Consequently, I am writing to establish whether you require the services of a <job title>.

Example 4:

I am currently studying at the University of XYZ and will be graduating with a <provide name of degree> in <Month>. My particular interests lie within <list interests> and I am presently seeking a position where I would have the opportunity to work within this exciting field. Please find attached my Curriculum Vitae for any Graduate roles you are presently resourcing in <list department or area>.

Example 5: Application to an agency or executive search firm
<Company name> has a superb reputation for working with and placing <job titles>. I am now eager to embark on a new challenge and I am writing to establish whether your clients may have a need for a <provide summary of experience>.

2. Body

- In the next paragraph, summarise your experience and articulate your most relevant experience in relation to the role(s) you are interested in.
- Next, list two or three achievements that would provide the reader with an insight into what the business benefit of hiring you would be. Provide them with a reason to contact you or

worst case scenario, keep your CV on file. Paraphrase your achievements; ensure you do not copy them directly from your CV.

- Review the company's website in order to ascertain what they look for in a potential employee. Then, convey those skills that will be of particular interest to the company and where appropriate, provide examples of where these skills have been demonstrated.
- Explain your interest in them as a company and what you feel you could bring to the organisation/department.
- Finally, what can you offer that is special or unique?

Example 1:

With over <xx> years' experience as a <job title>, I have a wealth of knowledge of <list core experience> in a highly demanding environment, coupled with <provide details of other areas of strength>.

My career highlights include <list two/three achievements> ...

I possess strong <list one/two core skills> with a proven ability to <provide examples of how/where you have demonstrated these skills>. I am recognised for <unique selling point>.

Example 2:

You will see from my enclosed CV that I am an experienced <job title> with <summarise experience>.

In my most recent roles, I have utilised my skills and experience to <list specific examples of where you have demonstrated your skills>.

I am a performance driven individual with a proven record of achievement of <provide details of two or three achievements>.

Example 3:

I am a career driven, enthusiastic individual/graduate with a <list education details> from <name of university/college/school>. During my studies, I have found <name subjects> to be the most rewarding, and would be very eager to begin my training in one of these disciplines.

Having worked as a <job title> during the summer, I gained valuable commercial experience which has provided me with an invaluable insight into <elaborate on experience gained>. Additionally, I honed <list skills that they are likely to be looking for in a graduate>.

Whilst at school/college/university <list details of some of your responsibilities or achievements, anything that will provide a prospective employer with an insight into what your capabilities are>.

3. Concluding your letter

- In one/two sentences summarise what you feel you can bring to the company or department.
- State when follow up will be, if appropriate.
- Convey your interest in hearing from them and thank them for their time.

Example 1:

As someone who is <summarise core strengths>, I am confident that I would make a valuable contribution to <company name or department/ team name>. I would welcome the opportunity to discuss my application further and will call you on <date> to establish how best to progress my application.

Example 2:

I am particularly interested in a <job title> position as I believe that the combination of <list your strengths, main skills and experience>, will make a positive contribution to the success and profitability of <company name>. I would be delighted to discuss my application in more detail and I will contact you on <date> to establish a suitable time for a meeting.

Example 3:

As an enthusiastic, goal-driven individual, I believe that I can bring a fresh, innovative approach to <company name/department>. I would welcome the opportunity to discuss my application further and I look forward to hearing from you soon.

Specific Cover Letters

Specific letters should be used to respond to an advertisement or in response to an approach by a company, agency or headhunter. Perhaps you have been made aware of an opportunity through a friend or colleague or maybe it is an internal vacancy.

Constructing a specific cover letter

1. Reference

Where appropriate, make reference to the role you are applying for. When responding to an advertisement, there is often a job reference number. If no reference number has been supplied, make reference to the role they are seeking to fill.

A reference should appear directly after 'Dear Name'.

Example 1:

Dear Mrs Allan

REF: Job reference 34215

Example 2:

Dear Mrs Allan

RE: Vacancy for a Marketing Director

2.   Opening paragraph
- Express your reason for writing; include the title of the job and how you became aware of the vacancy.
- Next, express your interest in the company and the opportunity, and convey your knowledge about the company or reader.

The scenario will determine how you start your letter.

Example 1: In response to an advertisement

<Company name> is a consultancy that I highly respect and admire as you have a reputation for <provide details>. I am also attracted to your organisation as you are reputed for rewarding hard work and nurturing talent. Following your advertisement in the <name of publication> on <date>, I am writing to apply for the position of <job title>.

Example 2: In response to an advertisement

In response to your advertisement for a <job title> placed in the <name of publication> on <date>, I am writing to apply for the position. <Company name> is a company <elaborate on why you admire or respect them> and I would relish the opportunity to work for your organisation. I have attached my CV for your consideration.

Example 3: In response to an advertisement

Being a dedicated and highly diligent student, I am incredibly keen to develop my education by means of a summer internship with a prominent <industry> organisation such as yours. I consider myself to have all the experience and attributes that you are looking for, for the position of <job title>, which my enclosed CV will attest.

Example 4: In response to a contact

<Company name> is an organisation that I hold in high regard and hence my elation to be contacted by <contact name>, who advised me that you presently have an opening for a <job title>. I am confident that I have all the skills and experience you are looking for and I am pleased to attach my CV for your perusal.

Example 5: In response to an internal vacancy

Following the recent retirement of <person's name>, <person's name, job title> recommended that I apply for the position as <job title>. Having worked for <company name> since <year>, I have <expand on your understanding of the company and the role>. As my enclosed CV will attest, I have all the skills and experience that you are looking for and this would be a natural step up for me.

2. Body

- In the first paragraph, summarise your experience and skills most relevant to the role you are applying for.
- The advertisement will list certain criteria and job requirements; the subsequent paragraphs should detail how you satisfy or exceed those requirements.
- Paraphrase two or thee achievements that will provide a prospective employer with assurance of your ability to do this job. Do not copy these directly from your CV.
- Clarify your interest in their company and what you feel you could bring to the organisation/department.
- Finally, what can you offer that is special or unique?

Example 1:

As you will see from my enclosed CV, I was <job title> at <company name> where I was responsible for the <list main duties and responsibilities>. I have many years experience in <elaborate on your areas of expertise>, which I feel uniquely qualify me for this job opportunity.

Besides undertaking <demonstrate your experience and qualifications in relation to the role>, I have recently qualified as <qualification> with a degree from <institution>.

I enjoy working in the <name of industry> industry and feel I am capable of developing excellent rapport with the people I work with. <Provide details of what skills and strengths you have in relation to the job being applied for and provide examples of where you have demonstrated these skills>.

In addition to my knowledge of <areas of expertise>, I have other qualities that will help me succeed in your organisation. I have developed the ability to <provide details of other areas of strength>.

Example 2: In response to an agency/headhunting firm

I note the requirements of the role and am confident that my experience and abilities would enable me to make a valuable contribution to your client.

Currently employed by <company name> as a <job title>, I have <xx> years' progressive experience of <state your core competencies and strengths in relation to the role>. Additionally, I am recognised as <provide further abilities in relation to target position>.

My most recent achievements have included <provide two/three

achievements that demonstrate your abilities to perform this kind of role for a similar organisation>.

I am <expand on further skills and experience that have been requested in the job specification and provide examples of where these skills have been displayed>.

Example 3: Recent graduate

I am an enthusiastic, committed graduate who has recently completed a <details of degree>. Having successfully completed internships last year and studied intensively this year, I have developed a sound understanding of <elaborate on experience and knowledge gained that is relevant to the role being applied for>. This has been reinforced by my participation in extra curricular activities and my consequent flourishing achievements.

Being a <list some of your key attributes relevant to the role> individual with exceptional <list two/three skills necessary for the job in question (e.g. communication and financial skills)>, I would benefit from fresh challenges and would integrate well within your organisation, interacting with clients and personnel at all levels.

Furthermore, <list any achievements whilst at school, university or college that demonstrate skills that they are requesting>.

3. Concluding your letter
- End the letter by reiterating your desire for the role and the company, and your confidence in your suitability for it.
- Express when follow up will be, if applicable.
- Convey your interest in hearing from and working with them.

Example 1:

I am confident that my skills and vast experience of <summarise your experience> will provide a pivotal platform for undertaking this interesting and demanding role. I would welcome the opportunity to discuss my application further and will call you on <date> to establish when our schedules will permit a face-to-face meeting.

Example 2:

In summary, I am attracted to the variety that this role will afford me and I would relish the challenge. As a result of my <elaborate on experience>, I firmly believe that I would make a valuable long-term contribution to <company name>. I would welcome the opportunity to meet with you and will call you on <date> to arrange a suitable time.

Example 3:

The honour of an internship with <company name> would hone my existing knowledge and experience whilst providing a more detailed insight into the world of <industry>. I am confident that I would offer a valuable contribution to <company name> and would welcome the opportunity to attend an interview.

Example 4:

With a studious disposition, entrepreneurial flair and with the capacity to easily absorb knowledge, I am confident that I am equipped to undertake any task presented in a professional and efficient manner. I would value the opportunity to discuss my application in more detail and I look forward to hearing from you.

Example 5: Internal opportunity

Having worked for <company name> for several years and closely with <person's name>, I have carried out many functions of the role in question and I feel that this would be a natural next step for me. I am confident that I would excel as the new <job title> due to my ability <list one/two reasons>. I would welcome the opportunity to discuss my application further and I will call you on <date> to discuss.

Summary
- Personalise your letter.
- Make your first sentence memorable, enticing them to read more.
- Keep it professional and concise.
- Express your reason for writing.
- Demonstrate a knowledge of the company as this helps to build rapport with your reader and displays enthusiasm.
- Explain your background, experience and how you can contribute to the company at this particular time.
- Summarise your experience. Include your most relevant skills and emphasise your most significant achievements i.e., those most appropriate to the job being applied for.
- Highlight the most important points from your CV.
- A cover letter should compliment your CV and not duplicate information from your CV, so reword sentences – do not copy sentences verbatim from your CV.
- Persuade the employer that you are confident you can do the job.
- Convey enthusiasm as enthusiasm sells.
- Keep the content relevant to your target position.
- Explain what appeals to you about both the role and the company.
- Provide demonstrable examples of what you can bring to the company and what the benefit in hiring someone like you would be.

- State when follow up will be. This will help set you apart from other applicants and will show your enthusiasm for the role.
- Diarise a follow-up date so you don't forget to follow through.

Full examples can be found here:
https://www.thecvdoctor.co.uk/how-to-write-an-impressive-cv.
Password: Impr3ss1ve

CHAPTER 26

Specific Cover Letters
That Have Worked

If you get your cover letter right, you will dramatically increase your chances of being invited to interview. The purpose of this chapter is to provide you with an appreciation of how to analyse a job specification, advertisement or similar; the art of mirroring; and how to go about constructing an interview-winning cover letter based on what is required. Four real-life examples of specific cover letters that have been successful are explored and analysed.

Recruiters screening CVs do not always fully understand the role they are trying to fill. They are working from a hiring authority's wish list of what their ideal candidate is and this is what the recruiter has to work with. Your job is to make their job as simple as possible; this means ensuring that your relevant skills and experience stand out on your cover letter. This way, you significantly increase your chances of being short-listed.

Four cover letter examples will now be discussed in detail. In each scenario, the original job specification (amended slightly to protect the identity of the company) is provided together with the actual cover letter that was sent. Finally, commentary of why the letter worked. In each example, focus is on emphasising skills and experience in relation to the person specification.

The first two examples are in response to an advertisement; the third is in response to an internal vacancy; the fourth example is a letter written by a candidate looking to be accepted onto a course.

Example 1: Andrea Smith
Andrea is seeking to secure a graduate trainee position with a major

investment bank or hedge fund. An executive search firm has been retained to identify potential candidates on behalf of their client and Andrea needs to convince the search firm that she is the right candidate for the programme.

Job title :   Graduate Programme

Company: Alexander Executive Search Ltd

Job description : The individual will create and compile presentations for clients; examine data and trends within the emerging market space specifically investment banking activity. A substantial portion of our transactions are cross border and the role will include travel to our key markets including Moscow, Istanbul, Dubai, Warsaw and Athens.

Person requirements : To be considered the candidate must have an exceptional academic background, strong communication and presentation skills, be charismatic, entrepreneurial and a team player. Proficiency in relevant languages is required, as this individual will be expected to help service Emerging markets based clients. Should have strong knowledge of Microsoft Office; in particular Excel, Word and Visio.

Vacancy type :   Permanent
Job status :   Full-time
Closing date :   20/05/20XX
How to apply: Leading City-Based Boutique Financial Services Emerging Markets specialist Executive Search firm is looking for strong individuals to join the graduate training programme.

The firm works on a retainer basis for top tier Investment Banks & HedgeFunds within Emerging markets.

With offices based in London, Moscow and Dubai key areas of regional coverage are:

* Russia/CIS
* MENA/GCC
* Central & Eastern Europe
* Turkey, Greece & Southern Europe
* Sub-Saharan Africa

Assistance in obtaining a UK work permit will be offered to successful candidates if necessary.

This firm has one of the most competitive remuneration structures in the City whereby commission is based on individual and team based performance.

Alexander Executive Search Ltd
Tel: 0123 456 789
Email: gp@abcd.com

Breaking down what is required as per the job specification

The candidate **must have**:

- an exceptional academic background;
- strong communication and presentation skills.

The candidate **must be**:

- charismatic, entrepreneurial and a team player;
- proficient in relevant languages.

The candidate **should have**:

- strong knowledge of Microsoft Office; in particular Excel, Word and Visio.

It is essential that all the 'must haves' be covered, followed by the 'nice to haves'. If there is something lacking do not draw attention to it. Remember, this is the specification for the company's IDEAL candidate.

The next page provides the actual copy of the letter that Andrea sent as an accompaniment to her CV.

Ms Andrea Smith
3 No Name Street
Oxford OX2

1 May 20XX

Mr John Greene
Consultant
Alexander Executive Search Ltd
25 Fleet Street
London
EC4 1AB

Ref: **Graduate Programme**

Dear Mr Greene,

I am very interested in joining your client's Graduate Programme. I have been looking to secure a challenging and exciting trainee position within an internationally focused and dynamic organisation, where I might have the opportunity to progress and develop my skills. I enclose my Curriculum Vitae for your consideration.

I possess excellent academic credentials, as a graduate in Law and Business Management with an MBA in International Business and Finance. Currently, I am studying towards a master's degree in European Studies at a leading business school, which I will complete later this year.

During my studies, I have had the opportunity to work with several Romanian organisations and successfully developed financial and x-efficiency programmes with them. I possess local connections within Eastern Europe (specifically the Russian and Romanian markets). I aspire to become a leader within an international business environment and feel that my language skills and understanding of other business cultures will be a great advantage as I enter the marketplace.

I am determined, confident and ambitious, with high levels of both academic and non-academic achievements. My communication and interpersonal skills are of a very high quality; I am diplomatic and good-humoured, maintaining a positive and supportive attitude with the ability to achieve desired results. I work well under pressure and excel in planning and organisation. A critical thinker, I am a highly capable decision-maker with excellent analytical and problem solving skills. My IT skills are strong, as well as my ability to confidently present information clearly and concisely to an audience.

I possess a genuine passion for business and some knowledge of the investment markets. I place a high value upon teamwork and the development of good working relationships with colleagues and clients. I enjoy travel and would embrace the opportunity to work internationally and work with global business leaders.

I feel that my experience and abilities would provide a positive influence within a forward thinking organisation and I would welcome the opportunity to discuss my interest further. Should you require any further information please do not hesitate to contact me.

Yours sincerely

Andrea Smith
Enc CV

Analysing the letter

Andrea begins her letter by expressing her interest in the organisation; even though she does not know who the client is, she draws upon some small details provided in the job specification.

In the second paragraph of her letter, Andrea quickly matches one of the core credentials – academic achievement and provides detail of her qualifications.

As the company has global operations, she then goes on to highlight her international experience with emerging markets and her international connections. She continues in the same vein by drawing attention to her multilingual capabilities and exposure to multi-cultural environments.

In the fourth and fifth paragraphs, she covers the two final requirements: computer literacy and an ability to work as part of a team.

She concludes the letter by expressing what she feels she can bring to the client and ultimately what the benefit to hiring her would be.

Outcome

All in all, Andrea expressed why she was a strong contender for this position and matched her skills and experience closely to the job specification, being sure to cover off each point. It is not surprising to hear that she was invited for interview.

Example 2: Shirley Simons
Shirley was applying for a role as a Guidelines Commissioning Manager in the public sector.

ABC NATIONAL INSTITUTE

Person Specification

Job Title	Guidelines Commissioning Manager
Team/Area of Work	Centre for Clinical Practice
Centre/Directorate	Centre for Clinical Practice

Knowledge, training and qualifications	
1. Requires highly developed specialist knowledge across the range of work procedures and practices underpinned by theoretical knowledge and relevant practical experience. • Masters degree or Doctorate, or • Equivalent level of knowledge acquired through experience and further training/development.	Essential
2. Familiarity with methodological approaches used to develop clinical guidelines or services.	Desirable
3. High level of interpersonal skills.	Essential
4. Ability to demonstrate the skills necessary to establish effective working relationships with a range of external organisations.	Essential
5. Ability to analyse complex issues, to think and plan strategically and to exercise sound judgement in the face of conflicting pressures.	Essential Essential
6. Ability to deploy resources effectively.	Essential
7. Understanding of the social, political, economic and technological context in which the NHS operates.	
8. An understanding of equal opportunities and the meaning of valuing diversity.	Essential

Experience	
9. Experience of managing clinical services in an operational unit or commissioning in the NHS.	Desirable
10. Experience of designing and leading on the implementation of significant change in clinical practice or service organisation, ideally across NHS units, within a local health community.	Desirable
11. Experience of managing project budgets.	Desirable
12. Experience of methodologies used in guideline development, e.g. literature searching, systematic reviewing, consensus methods and group working.	Desirable
13. Experience in working with a range of stakeholders in a health care setting.	Desirable
14. Ability to use standard Microsoft packages (including Word, Excel, PowerPoint, Access, Outlook) and websites.	Essential
Other attributes	
15. Effective and persuasive communicator demonstrating oral, written and presentation skills, with a high degree of personal credibility.	Essential
16. Initiative and judgement to be able to advise the Guideline Review Panels and the Centre Director on matters relating to the development of clinical guidelines.	Essential
17. Ability to engage effectively with clinical, academic and managerial colleagues.	Essential

Breaking down what is required as per the job specification

In the job specification it clearly states what is 'essential' and what is 'desirable'. As such it is important that Shirley specifies her experience and skills in relation to what is required.

The next page provides the actual copy of the letter that Shirley sent as an accompaniment to her CV.

Ms Shirley Simons
No 3 Apple Tree Road
Winchester SO53
Tel: 07123456 789
2 May 20XX

Mr Andrew Warton
Associate Director
ABC National Institute (ABCNI)
21 Short Road
London, WC1 5TA

Dear Mr Warton

Ref: Guidelines Commissioning Manager Vacancy

ABCNI is well known for providing independent, authoritative and reliable advice on healthcare issues. I have followed your organisation closely over the years and have been involved in the implementation of the ABCNI guideline for schizophrenia. As such, I have had first-hand experience of embedding ABCNI guidance into clinical practice.

In response to your advertisement for a Guidelines Commissioning Manager, I attach my CV for your consideration. I am a health professional with many years' experience working in the NHS. Additionally, I am from a nursing background and as such, I have the clinical experience, knowledge and maturity to understand the challenges that comes with a fluid organisation such as the NHS.

I possess self awareness, am politically aware and I have good analytical capabilities. I am an accomplished manager with a strong leadership ability and a demonstrable track record of managing the full lifecycle of several successful NHS projects.

My key skills and experience in relation to the role advertised are:
• currently studying towards a master's degree in Trans-cultural Mental Health;
• a skilled, persuasive communicator with well-developed interpersonal skills;
• effectively engages with colleagues from various professional backgrounds;
• experience of working with a range of stakeholders in the healthcare arena;
• adept at presenting complex information to multidisciplinary teams;
• familiar with methodological approaches used to develop clinical guidance;
• a thorough understanding of the social, political, economic and technological context in which the NHS operates;
• designing and leading the implementation of significant change in the NHS.

My most recent achievement was leading the development of the physical healthcare policy for my Trust. I recruited and chaired the strategy group, balancing the needs of various professional groups whilst keeping the physical healthcare objectives at the forefront. Currently, I am managing the consultation process for the policy, and identifying and communicating with stakeholders through various means. The policy is due to be launched within budget and on time.

I am passionate about improving patient care and raising standards, and as ABCNI is a learning organisation, I believe you would benefit from the level of experience and knowledge that I can offer to enhance your commitment to high quality clinical care. ABCNI exemplifies quality and excellence, which mirrors my career aspirations and is what motivates me.

It would be an honour to work for ABCNI, a highly pre-eminent organisation in the world of healthcare, and I would welcome the opportunity to discuss my application in more detail. I will call you on 16 May 20XX to have an informal discussion. In the meantime, please do not hesitate to contact me.

Yours sincerely

Shirley Simons BSc (Hons)

Analysing the letter

Importantly, the letter has been personalised and addressed to someone specific, i.e. Mr Andrew Warton. This not only shows that Shirley has taken time to research the company, it adds a personal touch and it also allows her to follow up her application.

Shirley begins her letter by demonstrating an understanding for and an interest in the company she is applying to. Skilfully, she also expresses previous exposure she has had with the company concerned.

She goes on to summarise her experience and background in relation to the role to which she is applying. In the third paragraph, she highlights some of her skills that are essential in order to perform the job and expands on her project management experience.

In paragraph four, she showcases additional skills and experience in relation to the job specification, making it very easy for a reader to see that she meets the criteria.

She subsequently highlights one of her most recent achievements, accentuating her ability to perform this role; it demonstrates the fact that she has achieved something similar for a previous employer.

Paragraphs five and six summarise what she can bring to the role and why the company and role appeal to her.

She concludes her letter by stating that she will follow up her application in two weeks' time. This shows she is proactive and again displays enthusiasm for the opportunity.

Outcome

This letter is well laid out and covers all the requirements outlined in the specification, so the person screening applications can quickly ascertain that Shirley meets the minimum criteria. Albeit Shirley lacked one key element, i.e. research methodology (which note, she did not draw attention to), she was still invited to interview.

Example 3 – Aidan Redbourn

Aidan currently works as a Production Manager at XYZ Dairy's Shipley site. He is now seeking to secure an internal position as Purchasing

Planning Manager.

The specification appears below.

XYZ DAIRY
PURCHASING PLANNING MANAGER

XYZ Dairy is a successful, expanding, independent cheese company, operating in the retail sector, dealing with leading UK and global companies. We are looking to recruit a Purchasing Planning Manager, the role to include:

Purchasing – To ensure that the company obtains the most competitive purchase prices for raw materials, packaging and other items by means of contract negotiation for others to order against that are commensurate with quality, technical and company purchasing strategy.

To ensure that stocks, goods and services are properly controlled, managed and accounted for at all locations so that they are available for use when required.

Planning – Responsible for accurate planning and forecasting you will play a vital role within the business ensuring efficient production, product quality and the highest levels of customer service via efficient purchasing, just-in-time management, stock control and good general operational planning.

Candidate – The ideal candidate will have experience in a purchasing/planning role in the food manufacturing industry, with chilled food experience. You will have excellent communication and negotiation skills, together with a 'hands-on' approach, able to plan and organise your workload effectively and have good IT skills.

If you are interested in this role
please pass your expression of interest to:
Kathy Henderson, Operations Manager by Friday 16 May

Breaking down what is required as per the job specification

The candidate **must have**:

- experience in a purchasing/planning role in the food manufacturing industry, with chilled food experience;
- excellent communication and negotiation skills;
- a 'hands-on' approach;
- an ability to plan and organise workload effectively;
- good IT skills.

The next page provides the actual copy of the letter that Aidan sent as an accompaniment to his CV.

Aidan Redbourn
20 Apple Tree Lane
Liverpool L8

Tel: 07123 456 789

2 May 20XX

Kathy Henderson
Operations Manager
XYZ Dairy Limited
25 Baron Road
Liverpool L7

Dear Mrs Henderson,

Ref: Purchasing Planning Manager

I am writing with reference to the vacancy for the position of **Purchasing Planning Manager**, and enclose my Curriculum Vitae for your consideration. I am a highly experienced manufacturing management professional, keen to further apply my skills and experience to the benefit of the business.

I have worked within the organisation for over 12 years and possess a breadth of experience in team and project management. I am capable of improving internal processes to create more profitable and efficient working environments. With proven success in purchasing of raw materials and packaging for the Shipley site, I am an experienced negotiator and troubleshooter. I am capable of maintaining a positive and supportive attitude with diplomacy and good humour in order to achieve desired results.

Recent achievements within the business include:

• managed change following the introduction of robotic line equipment, minimising disruption to production and maintaining high levels of staff motivation;
• liaised with contractors, engineers and suppliers during the building of a £1m extension;
• negotiated best prices for raw materials with suppliers;
• rationalised the usage of packaging materials, standardising the sizes of cardboard boxes across all three manufacturing sites, resulting in savings of around 10%;
• standardised the size of blue cheese manufactured across the three sites, resulting in a 10% reduction of waste;
• sold surplus milk securing profits of £120K during 20XX.

I am committed to achieving business targets and the continuous development of the organisation. My experience and achievements would I feel, allow me to create a positive impact within the role of **Purchasing Planning Manager**, and I would welcome the opportunity to progress this opportunity further.

Should you require any further information please do not hesitate to contact me.

Yours sincerely

Aidan Redbourn

Analysing the letter

Aidan begins his letter by making it very clear what role he is applying for and very importantly, he has addressed the letter to the appropriate person.

He then expresses his breadth of experience with the XYZ Dairy; it is essential to highlight this point early on as it is likely that this position will be open to external candidates. Internal candidates are often favoured above external candidates for two reasons: one, an organisation that progresses one's employees is more likely to maintain a motivated workforce; two, hiring someone internally is the cheaper option, saving the company expensive finder's fees.

The job specification specifies that the ideal candidate will have experience in a purchasing/planning role in the food manufacturing industry. Accordingly, Aidan proceeds to highlight his purchasing experience within food manufacturing.

In the subsequent paragraph Aidan emphasises some of his recent achievements, providing his reader with demonstrable examples of his negotiation and communication skills, and his ability to devise and implement cost saving initiatives.

He concludes his letter by stressing his commitment to achieving business targets and developing XYZ Dairy.

Outcome

Aidan focused on articulating why he was a strong candidate for this position and ensured he matched his skills and experience closely to the job specification. A cover letter is a fantastic way of drawing the reader's attention to your suitability for a role. Not surprisingly, Aidan was invited for interview.

Example 4 – Sam Dube

Sam was seeking to secure a place on an MBA Executive Programme with a leading business school, despite having no first degree.

Specification

ABC UNIVERSITY

Master of Business Administration (Executive) Entry Requirements:
In order to apply, you will need to have a good first degree or a recognised professional qualification and at least three years' postgraduate work experience at a managerial level. If you have not completed a first degree but are able to demonstrate several years' managerial experience at a senior level, your application will be considered.

Should English not be your first language, you will need to demonstrate a high level of competence in English Language.

Breaking down what the university is looking for

The applicant **must have**:

- a good first degree or a recognised professional qualification. Alternatively, needs to demonstrate several years' managerial experience at a senior level;
- at least three years' postgraduate work experience at a managerial level;
- a high level of competence with the English Language.

The next page provides a copy of the letter that Sam sent to the University.

Mr Sam Dube
21 Cherry Crescen
London EC1

Tel: 07123 456 789

16/12/20XX

Mr John Saunders
Head of MBA Admissions
ABC University
5 Westwood Road
London SW1

Dear Mr Saunders

REF: Application for MBA Programme – Leadership and Governance

ABC University is recognised as one of the UK's most popular business schools and I would feel privileged to be accepted onto your MBA programme.

As you will note from my enclosed CV, I am an accomplished entrepreneur with significant work experience encompassing a performance record of starting up several businesses from scratch across a variety of industries and thereafter, managing them into viable, profitable concerns.

In XXXX, I founded Granada Travel and Tours in Gabon, a travel/tour company involved in selling airline tickets, tour packages, car and coach rentals. More recently, I set up the same in the UK. The company is now one of the UK's leading travel/tour companies and a provider of money transfers to over 80 countries.

I am incredibly ambitious and feel that in order to achieve my aspirations more rapidly it is important that I receive a formal education. The reason I have chosen to study towards an MBA is because I believe it is a premier qualification that will provide me with a theoretical knowledge that I can then apply to my business, it will develop my management and leadership skills, and it will provide me with a good understanding of various strategic analysis techniques.

Having researched the various MBA programmes, I am assured that ABC University would provide me with a comprehensive theoretical introduction to the functional aspects of business. The key features of the course that particularly interest me are 'Strategic Marketing Management', 'Corporate and Business Finance', and 'The Economic and Global Context'.

I am confident that completing an MBA through ABC University will increase the likelihood of me realising my ambition to stand for president of my country and to venture into media.

If you have any questions or indeed wish to discuss my application further, please do not hesitate to contact me.

I look forward to hearing from you soon.

Yours sincerely

Sam Dube

Enc CV

Analysing the letter

Sam has personalised his letter and has made it clear what course he is applying for.

He continues by expressing recognition of the University's impeccable reputation – flattery is always good.

In the second paragraph, Sam summarises his background and expertise, and goes onto to provide two examples to demonstrate this point in paragraph three. Using examples to demonstrate your skills or experience is very important.

In paragraph four he communicates why he interested in this particular course and what the benefit of completing the course will be.

He then compliments the University further and expresses how completing this course will improve his chances of realising his ambition. This formula is the same when applying for a position, i.e., what appeals to you about the company and the role, and what the benefit of hiring you will be.

At no point does he draw attention to the fact that he does not have a first degree and although applicants without first degrees will be considered, the percentage is quite small. The point to note here is how important it is not to draw attention to anything negative or to any competencies/requirements that you do not possess.

Conclusion

This letter was well laid out, not too wordy and it covered all the University's requirements as outlined in their website. As a result, Sam's application was accessed by the University's academics and he received offers from two of the three universities he applied to, to attend the course.

Summary

A strong cover letter will significantly enhance your chances of being invited to interview. Keep it personalised, targeted and relevant. A cover letter can be both the making and breaking of your application so spend time getting in right. Proofread it before sending it out and follow-up your application if that is what you proposed.

Further examples can be found here: www.theCVdoctor.co.uk with password: Impr3ss1ve.

Action Words

Accelerated	Applied	Boosted
Accepted	Appointed	Broadened
Accessed	Appraised	Budgeted
Accomplished	Approved	Built
Achieved	Arranged	Calculated
Acquainted	Assembled	Captured
Acquired	Assessed	Catalogued
Acted	Assigned	Categorised
Activated	Assimilated	Centralised
Adapted	Assisted	Chaired
Added	Attained	Challenged
Addressed	Attended	Changed
Adjusted	Attracted	Charted
Administered	Audited	Clarified
Adopted	Augmented	Classified
Advanced	Authored	Coached
Advised	Authorised	Collaborated
Aided	Automated	Collected
Allocated	Averted	Combined
Altered	Awarded	Communicated
Analysed	Balanced	Compiled
Anticipated	Booked	Completed

Composed	Debated	Doubled
Compounded	Decreased	Drafted
Computed	Deduced	Drove
Conceived	Defined	Earned
Conceptualised	Defused	Edited
Condensed	Delegated	Educated
Conducted	Delivered	Effected
Consolidated	Demonstrated	Elaborated
Constructed	Designated	Elected
Consulted	Designed	Elevated
Contacted	Detailed	Enforced
Contained	Determined	Engineered
Contracted	Developed	Enhanced
Contributed	Devised	Elicited
Controlled	Devoted	Eliminated
Converted	Diagnosed	Embedded
Conveyed	Directed	Emphasised
Convinced	Disciplined	Enabled
Co-ordinated	Disclosed	Encouraged
Correlated	Discovered	Endorsed
Corresponded	Dispatched	Enlisted
Counselled	Dispensed	Enriched
Created	Disproved	Ensured
Critiqued	Dissuaded	Eradicated
Cultivated	Distinguished	Established
Curated	Distributed	Estimated
Customised	Diversified	Evaluated
Cut	Documented	Examined

Exceeded	Gained	Instructed
Excelled	Gathered	Integrated
Executed	Generated	Interacted
Exercised	Governed	Interested
Exhibited	Guided	Interpreted
Expanded	Handled	Interviewed
Expedited	Handpicked	Introduced
Explained	Harmonised	Invented
Exploited	Harnessed	Investigated
Explored	Headed	Issued
Extended	Helped	Illustrated
Extracted	Highlighted	Imagined
Extrapolated	Hired	Implemented
Fabricated	Identified	Improved
Facilitated	Incorporated	Improvised
Familiarised	Increased	Joined
Fashioned	Indoctrinated	Judged
Finalised	Inferred	Justified
Financed	Influenced	Launched
Focused	Informed	Lectured
Forecasted	Initiated	Led
Formalised	Innovated	Leveraged
Formed	Inspected	Liaised
Formulated	Inspired	Licensed
Fostered	Installed	Linked
Founded	Instigated	Lobbied
Framed	Instilled	Logged
Fulfilled	Instituted	Maintained

Managed	Originated	Publicised
Marketed	Overhauled	Published
Mastered	Oversaw	Purchased
Maximised	Participated	Quadrupled
Mediated	Partnered	Quantified
Mentored	Performed	Raised
Merged	Persuaded	Realised
Minimised	Pinpointed	Received
Mobilised	Pioneered	Recognised
Modelled	Planned	Recommended
Moderated	Positioned	Reconciled
Modernised	Practiced	Recorded
Modified	Praised	Recruited
Monitored	Prepared	Redesigned
Motivated	Presented	Reduced
Navigated	Preserved	Reengineered
Negotiated	Prevented	Referred
Nurtured	Prioritised	Refined
Observed	Probed	Regulated
Obtained	Processed	Rehabilitated
Offset	Procured	Remodelled
Opened	Produced	Reorganised
Operated	Programmed	Repaired
Optimised	Projected	Replaced
Orchestrated	Promoted	Reported
Ordered	Proposed	Represented
Organised	Protected	Requested
Oriented	Provided	Rescued

Researched	Solidified	Tracked
Resolved	Solved	Traded
Restored	Specified	Trained
Restructured	Sponsored	Transferred
Retrieved	Stabilised	Translated
Revamped	Standardised	Travelled
Reversed	Stimulated	Treated
Reviewed	Streamlined	Trimmed
Revised	Strengthened	Tripled
Revitalised	Structured	Troubleshooted
Revolutionised	Submitted	Tutored
Revolutionised	Summarised	Uncovered
Rewarded	Supervised	Updated
Saved	Supplemented	Upgraded
Scheduled	Supported	Upgraded
Schooled	Surveyed	Used
Screened	Synthesised	Utilised
Searched	Systemised	Validated
Secured	Tabulated	Verified
Segmented	Tailored	Viewed
Selected	Targeted	Visualised
Served	Taught	Volunteered
Serviced	Teamed	Widened
Set	Tended	Won
Set Up	Tendered	Worked
Shaped	Terminated	Wrote
Simplified	Tested	
Sold	Traced	

Index